The Night Of The Possum Concert

And Other Comedies

The Night Of The Possum Concert

And Other Comedies

Charles Allbright

August House / *Little Rock*
PUBLISHERS

Printed in the United States of America
10 9 8 7 6 5 4 3

LIBRARY OF CONGRESS CATALOGING-IN-PUBLICATION DATA
Allbright, Charles W.
The night of the possum concert.
I. Title.
PN4874.A37A25   1987   814'.54   87-1473
ISBN 0-87483-028-1 (paper)

Cover design by Bill Jennings
Production artwork by Ira Hocut
Typography by Lettergraphics, Little Rock, AR
Design direction by Ted Parkhurst
Project direction by Hope Coulter
Author photograph by Andrew Kilgore

For Tracy and Bern and Paul

Contents

Sports

Holidays

Animals

Children

Red Faces

Olden Days

Journeys

Sports

Unsung Hero Puts Robinson on the Road to Fame

Reports of Brooks Robinson's induction into the Baseball Hall of Fame were interesting because of what the reports left out.

Take the matter of who got credit.

George Haynie received a lot of the credit. He was Brooks Robinson's American Legion baseball coach at Lamar Porter Field in Little Rock.

Also, Paul Richards. It was Richards who first managed the cub third baseman in Baltimore.

Others were mentioned, and numerous assists went to the Almighty.

It is fair to say that there is truth in all of this. Whatever, Brooks had to get up and give credit to somebody.

Yet not one mention has been made of the person who actually put him on the road to Cooperstown.

It is modesty that prevents us from naming that person outright.

Brooks Robinson was a floppy-appearing child.

He did his early growing up on Lloyd Court, where that short street slopes away toward downtown, just east of the Arkansas School for the Deaf.

The neighborhood had an older, more gifted athlete, who has gone widely unsung. Modesty prevents our naming that person outright.

"Get out of the way, Brooks."

He had showed up one more time, maybe seven years old, wearing a large baseball glove and a cap that sat wrong on his head.

This child was an embarrassment to serious ballplayers twice his age.

"Y'all playing catch?"

The big guys were playing catch, up on the "deaf school" grounds.

"Throw me one," the floppy youth said.

That lopsided grin ran off his face in a direction opposite

the bill of his cap.

We threw him one, being careful to make it under-handed, something a child could handle.

He zipped it back.

A big guy said, "Brooks, your mother is calling you."

He ran down the slope, across Park Street, pounding his fist in that large glove, a dutiful son heading home.

Much has been said about Brooks Robinson's ability to go to his left. As well as to his right.

Also up into the air.

And down into the dirt.

Nothing was said at Cooperstown about how fast he could run down Park Street.

"Mama didn't call me"—in a flash the boy was back, grinning an all-right-you-guys grin, massaging that glove.

With any other seven-year-old, the ruse would have worked again. Something about Brooks Robinson's grin did not allow that.

"Throw me one," he said.

We threw him another one. He could not play with the big guys, but it was clear he was not going away.

Those schoolgrounds tilt. No matter how gifted the thrower, a ball released in a game of catch frequently soared off in some weird direction. We found the same thing, inexplicably, trying to catch one. Just as often, the ball bounced stiffly off our gloved fingers, into Park Street, then started the long roll down to the foot of the hill at West Markham.

Pass out credit where you will. It was not George Haynie or Paul Richards or the Almighty who allowed Brooks Robinson to run down Park Street after the ball.

"Now you got to throw me one," he said, arriving back at the top, panting and grinning.

It was in catching our little rewards that Brooks Robinson learned to go to his left and right, and up into the air and down into the dirt.

Our advice to a child who would follow in the footsteps of this baseball player is that he start practicing at an early age. Practice grinning.

Third base will not be played in such a manner. But if you can grin like that, it won't matter.

Mrs. Spivey Pulls Ahead by a Number at Oaklawn

Randall Barker of Pine Bluff reports that his sister, age sixty-seven, went for the first time in her life to Oaklawn Park to watch the horses run.

"She went with other ladies for the experience."

The Pine Bluff ladies spent three hours at the racetrack, placing one bet.

"My sister's neighbor, Mrs. Spivey, sent two dollars along to be wagered in any way her friends saw fit."

After four races, Randall Barker's sister screwed up enough courage to go to a betting window.

She handed the two dollars over and said, "This is for Mrs. Spivey."

The man back there said, "What's her number?"

"Her number?"

The man said, "I don't want the name. I need the number."

Barker's sister was perplexed.

"I think it's six–ten," she said, giving Mrs. Spivey's address.

The man said, "Is it six or ten?"

"It's six. I mean ten."

Randall Barker says, "I thought you might want to share this system with the people of Arkansas. Number Ten won the race. My sister went back and they gave her something like fourteen dollars, which she considered amazing because Mrs. Spivey's name wasn't even written on the ticket."

The ladies are planning another trip to Oaklawn next year.

There is more inside information on how to win money at Oaklawn Park.

A Little Rock man, widely known in Arkansas business circles, went over there for the first time since new wagering procedures were installed.

"Do not use my name," this sportsman instructs. "I can't afford to be regarded as a fool."

He approached the window for the first race.

"I guess I was nervous about how to go about it. My program was folded wrong. For the first race I bet on the Number One horse in the second race."

He returned to his seat, kicking himself through the crowd.

Lo and behold, the first race was won by the Number One horse. This man does not remember the horse's name. It could have been Mrs. Spivey.

"In my confusion I won eight dollars and eighty cents."

For the second race, he approached the window with diminished trepidation.

"Number One across the board," he said, putting down a five-dollar bill.

The man back there said, "Across the board? You owe me ten more dollars."

Not wanting to appear a fool, the Little Rock man put down an additional ten dollars. He kicked himself through the crowd, back to his seat.

"In my confusion, I knew I had squandered my winnings from the first race, and more money on top of that."

Lo and behold, the Number One horse came in again. Through ignorance, having bet fifteen dollars across the board, this man collected seventy-seven dollars.

Even a blind hog finds an acorn sometime.

That should end the account. But it doesn't.

Having figured everything out, he spent the rest of the day losing his winnings, and a lot more acorns to boot.

Golfer Takes a New Look at Fishing

The No. 5 hole at DeQueen Country Club is what Mike Beltrani calls "a nice, comfortable" par four.

That is easy for Beltrani to say. He is a three-times city champion who uses no more than a seven iron approaching the 380-yard hole.

There is one thing about No. 5. Fly the green, or hit it and hop over, and a pond awaits the ball on the other side.

Playing a Sunday round with Lee Chadburn, Mike Beltrani hit the No. 5 green and hopped over.

His ball had covered the flag coming in.

"I knew exactly where it would be if it went in the pond," Beltrani says, recalling the situation. "I lined up and went down to the pond, but there was so much moss, I raked a club through there and just decided to go on."

Monday morning at work the loss bothered Beltrani. That was no ordinary ball in the pond behind No. 5.

"It was an orange Wilson Pro Staff 1, the kind you can see from anywhere on the course. Everybody's trying to buy those balls and they're very hard to find. I just kept worrying about it."

Beltrani is not a fisherman but he knows people who are.

"I called Scott Russell and asked to borrow a rod and a plug."

Russell couldn't believe it. "You're going fishing?"

Beltrani said, no, he was not going fishing. He wanted to get his golf ball back.

So at noon Beltrani left work at Hollis and Company, got a rod and plug from Russell, went home and made a peanut butter sandwich, then drove out to the Country Club and the No. 5 hole.

To say Beltrani is not a fisherman is an understatement. He told us he broke the "twine" tying the plug on. Twine has not been used in fishing since safety pins.

"I don't know what kind of plug it was, only that it was orange, which was just a coincidence, and it had hooks on it."

With his peanut butter sandwich in one hand and Scott

17

Russell's fishing rig in the other, Beltrani went to the pond's edge, lined up with the flag on the green, and started dragging the plug through the moss.

The plug was snuggled right up to the end of the rod.

"It picked up a bunch of moss and I slapped it on the water to shake the moss loose."

Beltrani raked the plug a second time, eating his peanut butter sandwich, picking up more moss. He slapped at the pond again, getting the moss off.

On the third slap the plug stopped dead in the water. "Shucks," Beltrani muttered, or something to that effect. "I'm hung up."

He felt a massive tug. The reel screamed, smoked, as line tore out from the end of the rod.

Beltrani couldn't believe it. He dropped his sandwich.

"I'd like to say I fought the fish for about twenty minutes."

He'd like to, but that isn't what happened.

"I grabbed the rod with both hands and started running up toward the green."

The fish was horsed from the pond.

"I turned around and there he was, jumping around on the ground."

Beltrani ran at the fish and "dropped" on him. It was here, on land, that the great struggle took place.

"He was on top for a while and then I'd get on top. I'd never seen a largemouth bass like that."

What the fish weighed before the wrestling match will not be known. But after Beltrani finally subdued the fish and got it into his car, and showed up in front of Scott Russell with it, and after he got the catch over to the *DeQueen Bee*, where J.R. McKinley had the bass photographed and Beltrani written up, after all that the trophy largemouth weighed more than seven and a half pounds.

"I used to not like fishing," Beltrani told us, "but now I love it."

He says that Scott Russell, sick about the whole thing, took off all that week to fish the pond behind No. 5 and didn't catch anything.

Beltrani went back later and found his orange golf ball.

Golfer Finds the Hole for Big Bass

Some of his associates were so stung by Mike Beltrani's seven-and-a-half-pound bass, they went to the game warden about it.

Beltrani caught the lunker largemouth while slapping a moss-covered plug at the surface of a pond behind the fifth hole of the DeQueen Country Club.

The man wasn't even fishing. He was trying to recover a lost golf ball. And he was eating a peanut butter sandwich.

The bass latched on and Beltrani ran up the green behind him, horsing the fish out in that unclassical manner.

"I never caught a fish as big as that one's tail," the great angler told us.

Naturally he is having the bass mounted.

The whole thing was more disgusting than some persons could take.

"A group of them went to the game warden and tried to make a deal," Beltrani confided. "You see, I didn't have a fishing license."

The proposed deal was that if the game warden would come down on Beltrani, give him big trouble and issue a citation, then the friends would get up the money and pay the fine. They had to get satisfaction somehow.

"It didn't work. Our warden said he'd have to stretch things—the fish was caught on private property—and, well, he just didn't go for it."

Anyway, when he got wind of the plot Beltrani didn't stand around.

"I'm ready for them. I ran out and got myself a fishing license."

Mike Beltrani's friends would pay good money to rent Jack Hankins for a day and set up a golf game.

We knew Jack Hankins, a son of Kentucky, in the Army. He hated the military life, hated being away from home where he fished every day, and he hated any suggestion that might make his service time pass more tolerably.

He hated whoever got up that golf game, hated the bus ride to the course—and if anybody thought he actually was going to play, then that person was a fool.

Private Hankins, who had never played golf, tagged around for two holes. On the third tee, a 115-yard par three hole, he borrowed a ball, borrowed somebody's driver ("No! Jack! Don't!"), and wearing slick, leather-soled shoes addressed the ball and unleashed a mighty swing that looked like somebody falling off a house.

The ball hit one golf bag, three trees, seven or eight boulders, two cartpaths, assorted other items of landscape that were struck too swiftly to be identified, and about thirty seconds later one final object—the flag on the green, which Private Hankins's borrowed ball hit squarely and fell into the hole.

He threw the club down, saying, "What the hell is there to that?" and left the course in disgust.

Beltrani could say, "Yeah, but was he eating a peanut butter sandwich?"

Some Helpful, Fatherly Fishing Hints

We have here a letter from some friendly fishing tackle folks.

The letter is addressed "Dear Dad" and suggests that if we drop enough hints around we might get that fishing equipment we've been wanting for Father's Day. "And what could make a better present than landing that special bass?"

Coincidentally, we have been finishing up our findings about bass fishing.

Our research covers years of diligent study.

The dollar investment peaked at an uncertain figure. In the flush of expectation, a dedicated fish researcher lays down four dollars for something that looks like a frog with wings—a "sure-fire bass killer"—and then forgets how he explained it later.

We have a closet full of frogs with wings.

But now our research is complete.

Once and for all, when do bass bite and when don't they? What is the perfect time to get the "big fellows?"

Bass are said to strike hardest at daybreak and then again at dusk.

"Hold onto your hat!" the man at the dock says, ringing up his rental charges.

But we have not found this to be the case.

Our experience is that bass strike very poorly at daybreak.

They will not bite anything at dusk.

This pattern begins several hours before sunup and continues until midnight.

Bear in mind that this is the "big fellows." We know nothing of the "little fellows." Let them stay wherever they have been staying.

The inexperienced angler asks, "What about cloud conditions?"

Our documentation shows that there are two unproductive times to fish for bass:

1. Clear days.

2. Overcast days.

The bass is sensitive to weather changes. Let a cloud appear and he lurks near the bottom, disinterested in everything.

Clear the sky and a bass won't come up at all.

This applies to both daytime and nighttime fishing.

Mosquitoes, on the other hand, feed right on around the clock. Our recommendation is that during the conditions described, serious fishermen should leave their fishing tackle at home and fill the boat up with bug bombs.

"Was the wind blowing from the East?"

Yes, it was.

Also the wind was blowing out of the West.

As well as from the North.

We have been out there when waves were washing up on all four banks simultaneously. Holding onto our hat. And to both sides of the boat.

Bass simply will not bite when the wind is blowing from any of these directions.

Calm days are worse. Let the lake turn to glass and a bass would not bite if you offered him a ten-dollar bill.

In short, choose another time.

To conclude, the perfect time and condition for landing the "big fellows" is reached through the process of elimination.

Choose a day on which sky conditions more or less defy description.

The wind should be blowing straight down.

Launch your boat between midnight and 2:00 a.m.

On some undiscovered lake in the wilds of southwest Brazil.

Take along that fishing tackle you've been wanting for Father's Day. If you don't get it, take ours.

The Mystery of the Dehydrating Fish

In a cottage at Choctaw, near the western end of Greers Ferry Lake, Mrs. Joe Fugate admired a large bass newly mounted on a board over the fireplace.

A metal plate identified the angler who hauled the fish in, and gave the bass's weight as six and a quarter pounds.

"I'll bet he's proud of that," Mrs. Fugate said, referring to her hostess's husband.

The hostess smiled.

Mrs. Fugate read the weight again. "Six and a quarter pounds. My!"

Her hostess said actually that was known as "adjusted accurate" weight. She didn't understand completely, but her husband had been patient enough to explain it to her.

"When he brought the fish in it weighed four and three-quarter pounds. He said a fish that size dehydrates in a hurry—every fisherman knows that. So when he caught the fish it had to weigh at least five pounds."

The trouble with that, her husband explained, was that fish do not come out of the lake weighing exactly five pounds. That figure itself—"5 lbs."—would lack a great deal of credibility stamped into a metal plate beneath a fish.

Besides, it was quite warm that day. Dehydration probably had shrunk the fish up from no telling what actual weight.

In the interest of credibility, the angler determined that his four-and-three-quarter-pound bass actually weighed six pounds.

His wife protested, "But if five pounds doesn't look right, wouldn't *exactly* six pounds look just as phony."

He thanked her for that.

"You're right. We'll make it six and a quarter."

If we are not mistaken, it is "adjusted accurate" height that Bozo uses in interviews with his little television pals.

Bozo says to a little pal: "Boy! You're really tall to be so short!"

A taxidermist told us once that some fishermen achieved "adjusted accurate" weight scientifically, with the help of BBs and buckshot.

He produced a quart jar that almost couldn't be picked up with one hand.

"Some people think I just dip these fish in something, then mount them on boards."

His BB and buckshot collection was taken from fish he had mounted.

It made no sense to him.

"Within the realm of reason, I'll put any weight a man wants on his plate. It's his fish, and he ought to be happy with it."

He conceded that some realms exceeded reason.

"Now and then a guy comes in so excited about his catch, he expects you to look at a bream and call it a shark."

Some Fish Seem to Grow Faster
Out of the Water

Fishing near Hickory Nut Mountain on Lake Ouachita, Homer Cathy landed a largemouth bass that weighed in the neighborhood of two pounds.

"Actually, he might have gone closer to three"—that's the way Homer modestly described the fish to his brother, Nance Cathy, in a call to Memphis.

Homer and Nance Cathy have another brother, Don Cathy, who lives near Harrison. These folks all touch base by telephone on holidays such as the Fourth of July.

"Did you hear about Homer's bass?" Nance asked brother Don in the call from Memphis to Harrison. "Went right at four pounds."

They had a good visit, then Don Cathy signed off—"I guess it's about time for me to call Mom and Dad."

And so the nice day went.

Just before bedtime on the Fourth of July, Homer Cathy got a telephone call from his father, John T. Cathy, who lives down the block in Little Rock.

"Son, I've just been talking to your brother Donald."

Yes, sir.

"That five-pound bass of yours—is that the same fish you caught when we were fishing off Hickory Nut Mountain?"

Yes, sir.

"Nice going, son."

The largemouth bass is known for its rapid growth, especially on dry land.

Nobody is more helpful in observing these hefty weight gains than an alert taxidermist.

We know a Little Rock man who caught a largemouth and took the fish to be mounted.

A few days later, the taxidermist called.

"Your fish is ready. I'm getting ready to put the information plate on the board, and I can't remember whether you said he weighed five or five and a half."

When the fisherman did not answer in a hurry, the

taxidermist said, "He looks more like six to me."

In the interest of accuracy, the men settled on an average. They made the bass six and a half.

Walter Gancarczyk, who owned Spillway Landing on Lake Ouachita, once saw a bass double its weight before his very eyes.

"This fellow from Texas came off the lake with one fish, about three-quarters of a pound, and started pouring his kid's BBs into the bass. Put three boxes in there. Then he told the kid, 'Son, go get your mother.' "

The mother came and, under orders, held the bass up with her thumb in its mouth—"Get a feel of that," her husband directed.

It was an arm's-length, nose-holding performance. The loaded bass flopped once and fell free, back into the lake.

This is not a good summer for largemouth bass.

None of the expert fishermen we know has caught anything to speak of. If you can't speak of it, why go?

One expert, however, did catch something to shout about.

On the stream bank above Lake Maumelle he hauled in a sizable grindle. The grindle is a cross between an alligator and an army boot.

This grindle flopped into the fisherman's open tackle box and within five seconds was adorned with two dozen artificial baits.

Then he flopped back into the water, broke the line and took off.

The expert fisherman stood there on the bank and shouted plenty.

Dad Misses a Chance for Tryout

For several days last week an advertisement in the sports pages said that the Saskatchewan Roughriders of the Canadian Football League would hold tryouts Saturday.

Athletes showing up would have shots at joining the professional football team as wide receivers, quarterbacks, running backs, defensive backs, and linebackers.

Jamey Mullins, eight, of Little Rock has a young friend whose dad prepared to participate in the tryouts.

Jamey confronted his own dad about it. The youngster's mother, Helen Jane Mullins, provides us with the conversation.

"Dad, you're always saying you could play pro ball. Why don't you go try out?"

Dad said, "What day is that?"

Jamey said, "Saturday."

Dad said, "I would but I have to go out of town."

Jamey said, "What town are you going to?"

Dad said, "I have to go to Memphis."

The Roughrider tryouts were in Crump Stadium, Memphis.

Helen Jane Mullins says, "By the time I got Jamey calmed down his dad remembered that it wasn't Memphis he had to go to. It was Texarkana."

A brilliant career choked off by the fell clutch of circumstance.

We know how Jamey's dad must feel.

Our own career as a Tough Guy fell victim to blatant discrimination.

The announcement for the Central Arkansas "Toughman Contest" said the sporting event was open to "truckers, construction workers, policemen, jocks, factory workers, bikers, bouncers, and brawlers."

These men would bash away at each other until finally only one Tough Guy was left standing in the ring.

We complained to an acquaintance that no room was made for columnists. The promoters knew it would not be a pretty thing to see.

"Wait a minute," said the loud-mouthed acquaintance, reading the ad. "This says it's also open—and I quote—to 'any guy who thinks he's tough.' "

What were those dates again?

"It starts Friday," the acquaintance said.

We had to be in Memphis and Texarkana that night.

Holidays

Hog Jowls Make Holiday Dinner Authentic

Three weeks later, they are still talking about Mrs. Lloyd Hopkins's authentic Down South New Year's Day dinner.

They are talking as far north as Canada, to which most of the guests have fled.

That was a meal to remember.

Lloyd and Bea Hopkins live at Lakewood House at North Little Rock.

On New Year's Day, Mrs. Hopkins got her family together, two sisters from Ottawa and one from Mountain Home, and the husbands of two of them.

A ritual dinner for seven.

"They wanted to learn everything they could about Southern culture and traditions."

So Bea Hopkins set about preparing the New Year's Day dinner in the most authentic way possible.

There was a problem.

Hog jowls.

Bea Hopkins is from Canada, herself, having moved south only seven years ago. She wouldn't have known a hog jowl if somebody handed her one wrapped in cellophane.

Then she would have dropped the thing and run.

Her husband, Lloyd, a native New Yorker, didn't know a hog jowl from a hoedown.

On paper, Mrs. Hopkins prepared her dinner menu.

"I was told that to make the meal authentic we had to have hog jowls and black-eyed peas. Also turnip greens and cornbread. Along with cole slaw and fried pies."

The hostess arranged for all the other foods, and then presented herself to a man in the meat department at Skaggs Alpha Beta.

"I'd like seven hog jowls, please."

The meat man acquired a funny expression—"Ma'am?"

"Seven hog jowls."

Hearing her own words, Mrs. Hopkins experienced a sinking feeling.

"You would not believe the expression on the man's face.

It was utter disbelief. Then he began to collect himself. He was such a nice man."

You see, Mrs. Hopkins, late of Edmonton, Alberta, thought that everybody at her table got a hog jowl. One whole jowl to the plate. Quite a rich tradition.

"I assumed that this was the meat part of the meal, served separately."

(We asked Mrs. Hopkins how she had planned to cook the seven hog jowls. She said she hadn't gotten around to that part yet.)

The most tactful part of the meat man's explanation was the part he left out—how seven hog jowls cooked with black-eyed peas would feed the Canadian army.

"Ma'am, you see, the jowl is used only for flavoring."

So Bea Hopkins canceled her large order and took home one piece of hog jowl for eighty-nine cents.

The one time she actually set eyes on the jowl, and that briefly, was when she unwrapped it and, averting her gaze, let it drop into the crockpot.

It would have fed the Canadian army.

"Everybody hated the meal."

It never got clear what was the worst, the black-eyed peas, or the turnip greens, or maybe the vinegar—"this vinegar that you pour on, it comes off of some kind of Southern peppers."

Everybody agreed on one thing. Hog jowl itself was terrible.

They agreed on one other thing.

Mrs. Hopkins says proudly, "They hated the meal, but everybody absolutely loved the tradition. I don't know when we've all had such a good time together."

They'll get to enjoy it again. Just before everybody sat down to eat, a hidden tape recorder was turned on.

It contains more gags per minute than any recording in history.

Our hope yesterday, and pervasive wish, too, was with a woman who moved down recently from Massachusetts.

Monday she telephoned, getting ready to spend her first New Year's Day in Arkansas.

She did not want to start out by doing something dangerous.

"I know I am supposed to fix this special food for New Year's Day, but I am not certain about the instructions."

It was the black eyes that bothered her.

"Is it black-eyed peas and hog I'm supposed to fix? Or if it's black-eyed hog, what kind of peas?"

Mrs. Edward Vance was picking up her black-eyed peas at Brinkley when a young woman came scouting through the canned goods.

The grocery store aisle was crowded.

"This customer said my peas were what she was looking for, but obviously she was not enthusiastic about buying them."

The younger woman asked, with an accent not native to Monroe County, "Do you know if it's permissible to substitute, oh, something like green beans?"

Mrs. Vance got no chance to answer.

Another woman in the aisle hooted, "Honey, if you don't know better than that, it don't matter *what you eat!*"

All Praise Father and Grandmother of Our Country

As faithfully as possible, Lawanda Rule recorded a conversation as it occurred Wednesday morning as two men rode up an elevator in the Union National Bank Building.

One man said to the other, "Do you know what today is?"

"Today? Today is Wednesday."

"Yes, Wednesday. But what else?"

"Let's see. It's the day before the Razorbacks go out to Lubbock to beat Texas Tech and get ready for Houston."

The questioner was patient. "What else is today?"

The second man said, "Actually, today is the day I've got to get off of this elevator." Which he did.

As the door closed, the questioner spoke as though to a vast body of citizenry.

"Today is George Washington's birthday."

Lawanda Rule, the only other passenger, had an urge to get off between floors.

"People have just completely lost sight of it," the man said.

The elevator stopped. He got off, mumbling, "First in war, first in peace, and the first president to have his birthday moved to the weekend."

Moving birthdays around cannot enhance the study of history. Important things become fuzzy.

Jason Stevenson, age six, came home from school in North Little Rock asking his older sister whether she knew why we had George Washington's birthday.

Lauren Stevenson, nine, said, "Because George Washington is the father of our country."

Then it was her turn.

"Tell me, Jason, why do we have Abraham Lincoln's birthday?"

Jason thought he knew.

"Because Abraham Lincoln is the grandmother of our country."

In years past—quite a few years past—schoolchildren sat

33

at their desks in February and drew pictures of these two presidents.

George Washington drawings featured cherries.

Abraham Lincoln drawings featured Adam's apples.

These two great men looked either to their left or right, in profile, as though posing for coins.

Sometimes a boat was drawn under Mr. Washington. He looked away into river mists.

Always Mr. Lincoln looked away into the mists of years. His vision was impaired as a youth, they said, because he studied so late into the night, ciphering on the back of a shovel, having only the light of a fireplace.

Now they have changed their minds about that. Now they say the eyes are strengthened by working in poor light.

Look at a penny. It is clear that Abraham Lincoln was seeing further than anybody else.

But the main thing about these two men, American presidents, was that they were honest.

Tell the truth, children.

"Father, I cannot tell a lie. I chopped down the cherry tree."

For his honesty, young George was rewarded with only a minor thrashing. And probably no Grape Nuts Flakes before he went to bed.

Young Abraham walked nine miles from the log cabin, most of it through the woods, and a lot of it after dark, to return three cents to a merchant who had given him too much change.

On the McGehee schoolground, why Abraham did not discover the overpayment until he got all the way home was the subject of some argument, and more than one fistfight.

It is no bad thing when children put up their dukes over which of their presidents was greater.

The story is told that a late twentieth-century president, when confronted as a youth about a chopped-down tree, replied, "Daddy, I cannot tell a lie. Maybe I did, and maybe I didn't."

But those of us who are true patriots do not doubt. We do not rail at fuzziness. Everything is going to be all right.

Because here is February again. And we remember that George Washington and Abraham Lincoln were the father and grandmother of our country.

Saying "I Love You" Isn't Easy

It is the late afternoon rush hour at the TG&Y store, Valentine's Day. Last-minute shoppers jam elbow to elbow at the diminishing cards display.

This is no easy thing, saying I love you.

"I'll bet he doesn't give me one," a young lady half-whispers to her friend, nervously picking up a card.

The friend is a true friend, and says, "I'll bet he does, too."

"Well, anyway. I'll get him one that doesn't say anything."

It is no safe thing.

The men shoppers, all of them, are standing at the mushy cards. All are avoiding eye contact of any sort. Most of them shuffle. No nonsense love for them. They are after the big red cards, hearts and lace and foil.

"TO THE ONE I LOVE." The glossy thing swings open, producing a humpback lace doily from the fold. The doily is shaped like a heart, more or less:

"This card is to let you know, even if I haven't told you so, how much you really mean to me, and how I really hope to be—YOUR VALENTINE!"

It is not possible, closing this sort of thing quickly, to get the doily back to its original state.

Professional writers of Valentine card verses share one essential piece of information. They know that another whole year has gone by and people have not been telling each other. Thus:

"I know, dear, I don't tell you often, but the blow I hope to soften."

People should tell each other more often. It would be easier than this.

Women shoppers. They are scattered half at the mushies and half at the nonsense cards.

"I am at your disposal," says a card illustrated with a kitchen garbage grinder. A woman puts it down and a man, having read over her shoulder, quickly picks the card up. He palms it and heads for the cash register.

Saying I love you is one of the tough things in life. Saying it sincerely, and still not being a fool about it. "I am at your disposal."

Here a man is replacing a card as though with tongs: *"My love for you is very strong—enjoy your VD all day long."* Either he is a man of sensitive nature, or it is too late in the day, here practically at supper time, for the card to have much meaning.

"Dearest Valentine. Will you be free Saturday night. I sure hope so because I'm broke."

For MY AUNT. For MY BOSS. For MY NURSE. For MY FORMER HUSBAND. For MY FARMER HUSBAND. *"From your Loving Uncle on Valentine's Day, this is for Denise. And also for Denephew."*

It is no easy thing.

A man returns a card, looking simultaneously over both shoulders. His expression says to the other shoppers, "Nobody thinks I'd send a thing like *that,* do they?"

But the others do not see him. They are looking for cards, something to say, here at the last minute on Valentine's Day.

We love them all, these last-minute shoppers with the fragile and funny hearts in their hands. Sugar is sweet. Roses are red. And so are they.

Valentine, What's the Use of Waiting?

"If you love me and I love you, what's the use of waiting?"
Brazen!

Hazel Sandage bought that valentine. She went into town, into Heber Springs, and looked through all the valentines at Barnett's Drugstore, and that's the one she bought.

No fifteen-year-old girl in her right mind would put that sort of flaming language into the classroom valentine box. Not at Valley Special School. For all the world to see!

So she mailed it. On Valentine's Day, 1928, J.C. Harmon opened that envelope for the first time:

"If you love me and I love you, what's the use of waiting?"

This week, in their home at Little Rock, J.C. Harmon thanked his wife for proposing to him.

"Propose to you? I didn't propose to you!" Hazel Harmon said.

So J.C. got out the fifty-two-year-old valentine.

"If this is not a proposal I've never seen one."

He wondered how much she paid Barnett's for the card. Hazel said she paid a nickel.

Her husband said, "I'll bet you paid a penny, and then another penny to mail it."

You could not buy the valentine now for any price.

They waited three years. On July 4, 1931, Hazel Sandage and J.C. Harmon met in secret at the little store near Valley Special School, west of Heber Springs. Hazel's friend, Sylvia Varner, came with her. The three of them slipped over the Little Red River to the Pleasant Ridge community, and J.C. produced the newly bought license and what was left of five dollars he had earned digging post holes. That paid the justice of the peace.

Hazel said, "I wonder what Mother is going to do to me."

Her young husband laughed and said, "She can't do anything now."

The old school, the little store, the scenes of their youth now lie at the bottom of Greers Ferry Lake. The Harmons will not see those things again, and that is not easy.

But this Valentine's Day they have two children and three grandchildren and two great-grandchildren, and a golden wedding anniversary not far off.

"You know what?" Hazel Harmon says. "On our fiftieth I'd like to go to a church. Our own children could play the music, and the younger ones would be just about the right size to do something—and we could get married in a church."

J.C. Harmon says you'd think that one proposal would be enough—now here's a second from the same brazen woman.

He also says, reading from something in his lap, "If you love me and I love you, what's the use of waiting?"

Dreaded Fun of Easter Now Worth Admiring

As a youngster she dreaded the fun of Easter.

Her church used the season for its big push, recruiting new young Christians.

A lady we know was remembering how it was thirty years ago in lower Pope County.

"The Saturday before Easter our church always had this big Easter egg hunt. Everybody got invited, but especially big old boys you never saw around the church at any other time of the year."

The idea was that the big old boys would get caught up in the spirit of things and become young Christians.

She couldn't recall whose idea that was. Maybe the same elder who put on a Santa Claus suit and got his pockets picked at Christmas.

"Anyway, on Saturday morning before Easter we all stayed home and dyed eggs in the kitchen."

The memory of hot vinegar stung her nose.

"You dyed your eggs so you could recognize them later. Maybe it was how the colors streaked and ran. Or how you put the little designs on."

She remembered pressing a decal of a flowery cross on a pale blue Easter egg, holding it beneath a wet cloth.

Things got folded up under there and the flowery cross printed up like rabbit ears sticking out of a bush.

She could recognize that egg.

"You needed to know your own eggs because after the hunt all the children got their eggs back, more or less."

Overhearing this, a fellow observed that he hadn't eaten a hardboiled egg since the Easter he was five years old.

He remembered because that was the first year he got to wear long pants to the Easter egg hunt.

Also, that year he ate thirteen hardboiled eggs, which was about seven more than he could enjoy.

The last egg had been particularly green around the yolk. He had no idea how it got to the egg hunt, and more than fifty years later did not care to speculate about it.

At any rate, thirty years ago in lower Pope County, Saturday morning before Easter was spent dyeing eggs.

Then in the afternoon everybody went to the church.

The prospective young Christians were there early, not having brought any eggs.

Our narrator recalled:

"We turned all our eggs over to the adults, whoever the hiding committee was, and they hid the eggs."

Nobody peeped, except for the large visitors, who at that stage still were in the process of making up their minds about lifelong commitments.

Then an adult came back to where all the egg hunters were gathered and made informal remarks about what a lot of fun was had in the youth activities of the church.

The prospective Christians heard none of this. Their eyes were glued to specific tree trunks and jonquil clusters and rock piles.

"Go!"

At "Go!" she always did one of two things.

Either she pretended to be thinking about something else or, growing older, she contrived to trip over her own feet.

"With those bullies running around, my mother would have had to drag me to an egg and whip me before I'd have picked anything up."

Within minutes the prospective new Christians had virtually all the eggs rounded up and were back at the starting point, claiming whatever there was to claim for another year.

There was one exception.

She would always remember that just before each Easter egg hunt ended, the poorest child in town would somehow wander into the area of an encouraging adult and there—wonder of wonders!—find the biggest prize egg of all.

Remembering that, she loved Easter and she loved her church.

But First You Have to Figure Out Who Mother Is

It is time to remember mother.

If you can figure out who mother is.

Jamey Goodwin, five, of Hot Springs was getting his present ready for Mother's Day.

He asked his grandmother, "MawMaw, what's my mother's name?"

Mrs. Horace Thomas was careful to turn away and be businesslike.

"Why, Jamey, your mother is Mrs. James Goodwin."

Jamey kept wrapping. He said, "I thought so." Then he asked, "MawMaw, who is Marilyn Goodwin?"

MawMaw explained, "Marilyn Goodwin is the same as Mrs. James Goodwin. Don't you see, they're both your mother."

Jamey said he thought so.

The youngster kept wrapping.

He said, "MawMaw, if Mrs. James Goodwin is my mother, and Marilyn Goodwin is my mother, who is Marilyn Thomas?"

MawMaw Thomas explained, "Marilyn Thomas was your mother's name before she became Mrs. James Goodwin. In other words, she's your mother, too."

Jamey said he thought so.

"Now then," he said, tying the last string. "Who the hell's going to get this present?"

Dad, It Was the Thought That Counted

A fellow we know cannot get over what his children did for him for Father's Day.

It began with a surprise invitation.

His children, mostly grown, confronted him with guileful smiles and disclosed their plans.

"Dad, guess what? We're going on a big outing. It's all in your honor."

The man gulped.

They laughed and cuffed him playfully on the upper arms.

"It's true, Dad! Anything you want to do. We'll start the night before. Make it a big Father's Day weekend. What do you say, Dad?"

Dad was overcome by emotion and could not speak.

The young folks used the interval to formulate plans.

It was decided that Dad would get the biggest kick out of a trip to the lake. Plenty of fresh air, nothing for Dad to do but sit around and be treated like a king.

"No use protesting, Dad. It's all settled."

The plan, as outlined to Dad, was that he would go ahead and make the reservations—who knew more about that sort of thing than he did?

"Get plenty of cabins for everybody, Dad. Yes, and make yours the nicest. It's your outing, and besides we'll need a headquarters."

Food! What meal would Dad like most of all on his day?

While Dad made notes about reserving cabins, it was decided that his favorite Father's Day meal would be hot dogs *caramba!*

"Dad, are you getting this down? We'll need plenty of chili and chop some onions—get those hot onions—and melt cheese to pour on before the Tabasco. Then you'll want the Fritos to crumble on top of that—Dad, get about four dozen big wienies."

Dessert would be Danish wedding cookies.

Dad observed that with the aid of expensive drugs he had

managed some small progress with his ulcer, and that maybe he shouldn't—but they stopped him right there.

"Dad, if you can't treat yourself on your own day—make sure those are the all-beef franks—if you can't stop and enjoy yourself once a year, you're going to ruin this whole thing for everybody."

Dad apologized and said forget about him, he would skip the noon meal and fix himself a big breakfast.

"Breakfast!" they chorused, cuffing him gleefully, now in the ribs and on the ears. "Dad, you're going to sleep in on Father's Day. *We're going to fix your breakfast!*"

So Dad went on to the lake—the children stayed back to gather surprises—and got plenty of cabins for everybody, and purchased large stores of food which he managed to carry in six trips from the car to the headquarters cabin, feeling honored all the while.

At dark the children arrived, honking ceremoniously, and began unloading surprises—tape decks, loudspeakers, enough Black Sabbath and Grateful Dead music to keep a Father's Day Eve concert going until 2:30 a.m.

Next morning everybody slept in in honor of Dad, who was allowed to fix breakfast.

As he cleared away the dishes, the young folks left to launch the boat—"You just stay here and take it easy, Dad, while we feel out the water conditions."

The feeling out was completed by noon, at which time the young folks returned, famished.

While Dad cleared away the noon dishes his children napped briefly, being tired from all their honoring.

Then all went down and got into the boat.

Except for Dad.

"Dad, give us a good push off from the bank, and then jump in."

So Dad pushed and with a mighty leap landed knees-first on the bow of the boat, which did not budge from the bank.

The crunching sound practically made everybody sick. They were still shouting solicitations as they headed for open water, waving to Dad there on the bank—"Dad, as soon as you can walk, put something on those knees!"

"Dad, don't forget to check us out of the cabins!"

"Dad, it doesn't matter how you load the cars. Just throw our stuff in!"

"And Dad, take it easy and have a wonderful Father's"—
but by then they were out of earshot, having done all they
could do.

They found him in the late afternoon. Thin sunlight
slanted through the trees where he reposed, head back and
mouth open, in a folding chair.

The voices seemed to come from far away:

"Look at him. He's worn out from all the fun."

"Somebody get those flies away from his head."

"I can't wait until next year. It's a lot of trouble but Dad's
worth every bit of it."

Grownups Can't Get Over Halloween—Or Get It Over With Too Soon

Somebody is going to observe that Halloween is not what it used to be.

Somebody already has.

This fellow drew twenty cents' worth of Dracula brew from the coffee machine in the Vendateria and sat down to join a group.

"Halloween isn't what it used to be," he said, shaking his head.

"Heck, no!" somebody agreed.

The first said, "I'll never forget the time"—he started chuckling.

"I'll never forget the time we put the goat in the"—here he broke down.

The group would have to forgive him.

"This is going to kill you," the rememberer said. Everybody sat back and drank coffee in anticipation of being killed, being pretty well along the way already.

What this fellow would never forget, it turned out, was the time he and a friend tied a goat up in the basement of the church.

He had to be helped back into his chair.

A listener aroused himself from the dead long enough to ask, "What happened?"

The narrator raised his head from between his knees, near-faint from remembering.

"What do you mean?"

"The goat? When they found the goat in the church basement—what happened?"

"They made us take him out."

The one who would never forget shook his head. Under control again, he observed, "That goat."

Halloween is not what it used to be.

In the old days when the darkness of Halloween night

45

fell on the highway south of McGehee, only a fool would have got out there.

"They's electric wires all over the highway," a large and menacing teenaged boy told us privately.

"They's what?"

"Killer electric wires. Thick as snakes all over the highway. If you step on one of those naked wires you'll fry."

How we made it through that blackness to Bryan Junior Simpson's house and back, with both feet in our knickers pockets, is something that might be written up in an antigravity manual.

Next morning all the killer wires were gone. In the daylight you could see where they had been.

Having no enthusiasm for tricking and treating in the first place, Robert Mallory of North Little Rock decided to get the whole thing over with.

At 5:30 p.m. Mallory told his two sons to get into their costumes.

"Already?" said Bobby, eight.

"Are you sure?" said David, six.

The elder Mallory cracked his palms together sharply. "Right now! Let's go!"

The two goblins appeared at their first door, with Dad standing eight feet to the side, his arms folded.

A woman opened the door.

Nobody said anything.

Mallory instructed the goblins from the corner of his mouth, "Say trick or treat."

The goblins didn't say anything.

Mallory grew firm, commanding, "Say trick or treat!"

The goblins said feebly, "Trick or treat."

The woman at the door protested, "Boys, this is Sunday. Halloween's not until tomorrow."

The larger goblin said, "We know. Dad's making us do this."

Bored Relative Plans Way to Avoid Get-togethers

Our friend Reid insists that he loves his relatives as much as the next man, probably more, but he is on the verge of taking a position on holiday family get-togethers.

"Call me crazy," Reid says, "but I believe families can love each other without making each other miserable."

Reid is crazy.

"The problem is that nobody can admit he'd rather be somewhere else. It would seem ungrateful. You'd be a werewolf or something."

On Thanksgiving afternoon, Reid looked at his wife across a crowded room. For an instant, her eyes rolled back in her head.

Rolling his eyes in kindred anguish, Reid got caught by his older sister.

"I started to pretend it was the smoke. Or too much sage in the dressing."

Then Reid saw the flicker of a smile on his sister's lips.

"Her eyes rolled back."

Reid's sister was caught, in turn, by their father. The elder Reid turned to look out a window, into the yard.

"My dad loves to watch football on television. It doesn't matter who's playing—Manitoba versus the West Indies. But does he get to watch on Thanksgiving? No! We are all having too much fun."

It is not known whether Reid's mother rolled her eyes. She was upstairs, having collapsed from getting ready for all the good times.

For a moment on Thanksgiving afternoon, Reid thought of polling the two dozen family attendees. His wife read something dangerous in his face and, from across the room, shook her head.

Reid has a plan for Christmas.

"We have to figure out how to love each other, and spare each other at the same time."

Reid's plan entails writing an anonymous note.

"I'm going to write this note, not signed or anything, and

put it on the coffee table. It won't matter whose house we're at."

Reid's anonymous note will say, "They can't afford for all of us to be here."

He explains, "You see, this note will get picked up, and whispered around, and people will start saying, 'Well, far be it from me to bring hardships down on my family. I love them too much. And that goes for my in-laws, too.' "

Reid hates to think what will happen out in the driveway.

"It's going to look like a demolition derby, with everybody trying to clear out first."

Mrs. Reid does not like this plan. She likes nothing about it.

"You fool!" she said to our friend. "Don't you know somebody will pick up that note and recognize your handwriting? What about your Aunt Mae?"

Reid said, all right, he would type the anonymous note. Or get somebody else to write it.

"I'll get Dad. It was his idea in the first place."

No Good Answer to This Family Feud

A reader who signs herself "Never Bored" is scandalized that a man named Reid could use this space to make sport of traditional family get-togethers.

In truth, Reid was not making sport.

"The family that gets together regrets together."

Reid made up that holiday slogan right after his family's most recent Thanksgiving gathering.

Loved ones drove in from miles around, arriving with anxiety headaches, and broccoli casseroles tumped over in the car trunk.

Everybody was smiling, not counting the children, who were kicking each other.

"The only thing we won't do as a family," Reid said, "is spare each other."

He is looking into leasing a billboard for Christmas.

"The billboard will feature my slogan, and a large pair of praying hands to emphasize the religious feeling behind the message."

Never Bored concludes that Reid simply does not get into the spirit of things.

"If I knew who he is, I would consider inviting him to our next Thanksgiving family get-together, which is held annually in our home in North Little Rock. This year my husband and I had thirty-three family members, from ages five to ninety-two."

Reid does not understand that.

He points out that one of the greatest things the Pilgrims taught us to be thankful for, professional football, cannot be watched respectfully when a large number of loved ones block the television screen.

Or even one large loved one. His Aunt Mae alone took out both the Detroit Lions and the Pittsburgh Steelers, with one massive body block lasting the entire third quarter.

Never Bored insists it doesn't have to be!

"My husband is also an avid sports fan and this is a simple matter to handle. Just turn on any and all TV sets in your house, place the easy chairs in front of them, and this makes a perfect spot for the sports fans to watch [or sleep through] the games, and also keep out of the way of other moving persons."

Still Reid is skeptical.

"We have all grown up and gone separate ways. This doesn't mean we don't love each other. It means we just don't have all that much to talk about."

Reid made this observation to his brother-in-law. His brother-in-law nodded, saying he couldn't agree more.

"Then he told me about his rack and pinion steering."

Never Bored, with thirty-three houseguests, sees no problem at all.

"If one should become bored (heaven forbid!) or thrown with another relative one might want to avoid, then go to another room where the pursuit of other activities might be enjoyed, such as imbibing a few spirits or participating in a hot dart game."

Reid counters that his family has nothing to do with alcohol. Except for making jokes about it.

"My Uncle Fred always says, standing there in front of the fireplace, 'Well, I've always said, anytime you get as many as four Reids together, you ought to be able to find a fifth.' "

Everybody laughs and enjoys a new round of headaches.

Reid is grateful for Never Bored's kind invitation. He looks forward to attending with the thirty-three others next Thanksgiving, unless he is ill, about which there is a strong possibility.

Meanwhile the man is going through with his Christmas billboard, as well as a plan to leave an anonymous note on the family gathering coffeetable.

The anonymous note will say, "They can't afford for all of us to be here."

Reid wants to see how many can escape injury in the mass departure.

Ho Ho Uh-wah

Wayne Bolick got an early Christmas gift this year. Whoever thought up Santa Claus's telephone number—the one youngsters are supposed to call at University Mall—managed to miss Bolick's home phone by only one digit.

The Bolick home phone is 666–0040.

Santa's voice at University Mall can be reached at 666–0044.

Ho ho ho.

The University Mall telephone number is being advertised all over the place.

As for when the first call for Santa came, Bolick does not even remember any more. He works nights. But since that first call, they now start coming about 7:00 in the morning. They keep coming up to 11:00 at night.

Dozens of calls to Santa, all misdialed on the last digit.

The big trouble arises, Bolick says, when parents dial Santa's number (the wrong one) and then immediately jam the receiver against the ear of a child. The child is tongue-tied with wonderment.

A typical conversation goes like this.

Wayne Bolick: "Hello."

Parent, whispering to child: "Say something to Santa."

Bolick: "Hello?"

Parent, beginning to hiss a bit: "Is he on there? Go ahead and *say something!*"

As a rule, Bolick does not say hello a third time. He waits it out, visualizing a wide-eyed child, mouth open but nothing coming out, the telephone planted against a small ear.

Finally the parent who is responsible for this foulup loses cool and shrieks a command at the speechless child: "If you know what's good for you *tell him what you want for Christmas!*"

Child: "Uh-wah."

At this point the conversation goes down the drain in one of two ways.

1. The parent slams the receiver down and presumably begins giving the youngster a little Christmas what-for. Or,

2. The parent wrenches the phone from the child's ear

51

and for the first time speaks to Santa: "Who is this?"

"This is Wayne Bolick," says Wayne Bolick.

Some parents simply are not prepared to put up with Wayne Bolick, after all the trouble they have been to. They bang the receiver down, not wishing Bolick a merry Christmas.

Other parents start mumbling, sounding like their children, "Uh-wah...Who is?...er-ruh."

Bolick then is as cheerful as the hour of day or night permits.

"I'll bet you're looking for Santa Claus. His number is"— and then Bolick gives the shopping center number.

The Bolick household has tried to adopt an attitude about all this—ho ho ho.

"I don't want to disappoint any children, or frighten them, so for a while I made up my mind just to go ahead and answer the phone every time it rang by saying ho ho ho."

But something changed his mind.

"There is a very special message I want to give to the person who thought up this telephone number. In case he should call up, ho ho ho is not the message I want him to get."

Party Desperately Short of Waffles

It was during the time they traveled Europe and lived in Norway, that first year out of Harvard Law, before settling down to careers and family, that Steve and Janet Shults became addicted to waffles.

Norway because Janet's family is Norwegian.

For six months the young American couple worked on a dairy farm, living with the owners.

Janet Shults recalls, "We worked hard, but we also ate hard. In fact, we ate all the time—homemade delicious goodies like rolls, breads, cookies—and waffles."

They lived there through Christmas—"a time when baking is at its best, and waffles are in abundance. We often had waffles for supper (dinner), only to go to a neighbor's farm for a Christmas party and have them again."

Of course, the days of waffles and roses could not go on forever.

Back in Little Rock the following year, the Shultses were delighted to be invited to a waffle dinner party.

The party was at the home of Mark Lester and Jeanne Jackson, young married friends of the Shultses.

Janet Schults admits to being excited "that they liked waffles as much as we did. In fact, so much that they wanted to have a party just to eat waffles."

It was like the man who confessed to his psychiatrist, "I love pancakes."

The doctor said, "What's wrong with that? I like pancakes, too."

The patient exclaimed joyously, "You do? Then come over to my house. I have a closet full of them!"

On the day of the party Janet Shults skipped lunch—"in anticipation of waffles dripping with preserves and whipped cream."

Also going to the party were Tom and Debby Ray.

Janet Shults reports, "They didn't realize waffles would be served until we told them. It took some convincing— eating waffles for dinner—but by the time the party arrived they were as excited about those waffles as we were."

Tom and Debby Ray skipped lunch also. The foursome, the Rays and the Shultses, arrived at the party hungry enough to eat the doilies.

Excitement became uneasiness.

"The four of us wandered all over the house full of partying people trying to find those waffles. We couldn't find them. We couldn't even smell them cooking."

Uneasiness turned to anxiety.

"Tom Ray was eating all the peanuts and crackers in sight."

There comes a time when you must assert yourself.

Take the social bull by the horns.

Walk right up to the hostess and say it.

"Finally, out of desperation, we asked the hostess if she would be so kind as to point us in the direction of those waffles."

Jeanne Jackson's holiday expression glazed over.

Waffles?

"She informed us after a look of disbelief that there were no waffles."

No waffles at a waffle party?

"But that we could help ourselves to all the wassail we could drink."

The good news, for those who missed it earlier, is that this holiday season there will be free cab rides for persons who cannot drive home safely after going out and having too many waffles.

The messy scene can be avoided.

An officer stands there with his pencil and ticket book and says, "Sir, how many have you had?"

"Well, I had one plain and one pecan."

Officer: "Are you sure that's all? Your eyes look funny."

"Come to think of it, I also had a banana and two blueberries."

Officer: "Get in the back of the car."

This year it can be avoided. Before you butter that third one, call the special number.

How to Pacify a Pint-sized Nativity Star

We are indebted to John Malone for his outstanding report on how things went this year in the live manger scene at Pocahontas Methodist Church.

The role of Baby Jesus was performed by the now distinguished actor, Tom Riffel, age six months.

Patty and Kirby Riffel, parents of the star, sat enthralled in the congregation.

John Malone reports, "The Baby Jesus made it through the first half of the program in great shape. Then he became a little restless."

In the live manger scene, Mary was played by teenager Robyn Harris. When Baby Jesus began howling, Mary did what any young mother would do. She handed off to Joseph.

Joseph was, in fact, teenager Chad Couch. You don't get to be Joseph by being a dummy. Joseph handed Baby Jesus off to the nearest angel, in real life teenager Dawn Gutteridge.

Baby Jesus went around the manger like a hot potato.

Talk about a *live* scene!

John Malone says of the sound effects, "It was now a pretty even battle between the crying baby and the twenty little singers in the choir."

Here came the wise men.

"The gold, frankincense and myrrh were coming down the aisle."

Malone saw that one of the wise men walked a little ahead of the others, moving with the urgency of a greater wisdom.

"He went straight to Joseph."

And to all those of Pocahontas Methodist Church, what was the greatest gift of all?

It wasn't the gold. It wasn't the frankincense. It wasn't the myrrh.

It was the pacifier.

Overgrown Boys Keep Memories Alive

When it was over, and everything got still, some overgrown boys sat and talked about old Christmases.

"The Christmas I won't forget," one said, "was the year I got my bicycle."

He was ten. The bicycles were in the window of the Western Auto store. Two bicycles, identical.

He and his brother spent the days before Christmas walking back and forth to the store, looking in through the window, not saying much.

Christmas Eve the bicycles disappeared from the window.

"I got so excited, so scared, I almost choked," the overgrown boy said. "My nose started running, and it wouldn't stop."

He'd rather have kept those bicycles in the window, kept them there forever, than fight the fear they were going somewhere else. A dream has enormous value of its own.

On Christmas morning the bicycles were in his living room, gleaming in the soft light of the tree.

"That morning we left to visit relatives. It was a long drive, and I think we stayed about a week. I loved my cousins, but leaving that new bike just made me sick."

The old boys talked on.

"My favorite," another said, "was any Christmas I got a new football. There must have been about ten of those."

In knickers he was a football whiz.

"By the time I was eight I'd get out there in the yard, by myself, and have a gigantic football game. I played every position on both teams."

Not only that, he was also the radio announcer, describing fantastic plays as they occurred. It went on for hours.

"Charles, who on earth are you talking to?"—his mother had come unnoticed onto the front porch.

He turned red and said, "Nobody"—announcing under his breath that the teams were leaving the field for halftime.

"I sat under a tree until my mother went back inside."

The Christmas he was twelve he decided on Georgia Tech. He would go there and become an All-American running back.

The Christmas he was thirteen he flunked seventh-grade arithmetic. It cost Georgia Tech a great star.

He said, "On Christmas morning I still love to feel a new leather football. The seams are still stiff, and sort of ridged up."

And on the old boys talked.

"It was a Daisy pump," this fellow said, describing his new BB gun.

Some friends got Red Ryder models, the carbines. But his was the Daisy that you pumped by holding the knees together, getting in a semi-sitting position, and then pulling down, risking a hernia before each shot.

"That Christmas it snowed. I had never seen snow on Christmas before."

He went into some woods near his house and found an incredible number of small, yellow-breasted birds. Their food was beneath the snow. The noise of the hungry birds massed in the trees was unbelievable.

"I killed one hundred and twenty of those birds. I took them home in a tow sack and lined them up in the back yard, in rows, like a company of men. Then I went in and got my dad."

For a long time the two of them sat on the back steps, looking at the small birds. When his dad finally spoke, he said, "Son, what are you going to do with them?"

"I told him that if he would go back inside, I'd take care of them."

That Christmas afternoon he buried one hundred and twenty yellow-breasted birds in his back yard.

Then he found a rake. He raked until he could see no more red spots in the snow.

For more than forty years he had shot at no other creature. But there would not be enough years to make it up.

"There is no such thing as a favorite Christmas," another fellow said. "They are like your children. You love them all."

A woman came into the room where the meeting was being held, and said, "Charles, who on earth are you talking to?"

Now Christmas Will Also Mean TuTu, H.T. Magby

Whenever the Christmas season comes again, for as long as it keeps coming, we will think of TuTu Magby.

Her real name is Thelma Magby. She lives on Massie Street in North Little Rock.

We have never met this woman.

She gave to us the greatest Christmas gift of all.

A week before Christmas there was a letter from Mrs. Magby. And after that a telephone visit with her. From those we gathered the details of how TuTu and her husband, H.T. Magby, went looking for their Christmas tree.

The letter was full of cheerful spirits.

When she wrote it, when we talked, Thelma Magby could not know that she and her husband had gone looking for their last Christmas tree.

Tutu sounds a lot like MaGoo. Without her glasses, Mrs. Magby rates with the scouts at Little Bighorn.

As her husband drove that day, she spotted a sign that said, "Bill's Trees." Or that's how it looked to TuTu. An arrow seemed to point to the right.

The Magbys took off on a bewildering tree search that wound up many miles later, back at the same sign in North Little Rock.

H.T. Magby sat there and read the sign for himself.

He saw that the arrow pointed to the left. And the sign said, "Bill's Tires."

H.T. exclaimed, "Do you see what I have to live with!"

TuTu Magby held her head in her hands. Then she threw it back—"Oh, no!" TuTu, you've done it again.

The letter said, chiding herself, "I wanted somebody to know what a patient and understanding man I live with."

But that is not at all what the letter said.

What it said, as the days drew down at Christmastime, was "I love this man. And I love him for loving me."

H.T. Magby knew that.

TuTu Magby wanted him to know that she wanted the world to know.

59

So it was just right for us, this family misadventure, written in advance for publication the Tuesday before Christmas.

You see, H.T. Magby's exasperation was purely counterfeit. They drove away from the Bill's Tires sign a second time, going their way in laughter.

The notice of his funeral appeared in that same edition of the newspaper. The Tuesday before Christmas.

He had gone suddenly, on Sunday.

She lay in bed that Sunday evening, trying to make sense of things, and from somewhere it came to her—"Oh! I talked to the newspaper about our Christmas tree!"

But that thought didn't last long.

In this world there is not enough room to turn around.

Not enough dark closets to go stand in.

Not enough words to reach out for.

Because still a person must stand there, exposed to himself in the full glare of his own insignificance, the one who on another man's last day on earth was still in there making nonsense.

And not enough space to disappear into.

She called the morning after she buried him. The day after their Christmas story appeared.

"This is TuTu Magby."

The words were not easy. She started over.

"This is TuTu Magby. I wanted you to know something."

She said there were eight brothers and sisters.

"We talked it over. I wanted you to know that what was in the paper, that was just fine."

Animals

"Big Boy" Bests Ashley County's "Dog Man"

Hodge Phillips, the headmaster of Montrose Academy down in Ashley County, is known among his fellow hunters as "Dog Man."

This is because of Phillips's vast knowledge of dogs.

Ask any hunter in three counties. They will tell you, yes, old Hodge is something special when it comes to dogs.

Who else but Hodge Phillips would have left Dermott on a deer hunt Saturday morning with eight dogs in the back of his pickup truck?

Or maybe it was ten dogs.

Not counting Big Boy.

Up front in the cab with Dog Man rode his main dog, a two-and-a-half-year-old beagle, Big Boy.

This group took Highway 208 out of Dermott, bound for deer camp where an assortment of expert deer hunters waited for the dogs.

As they rode, Dog Man and Big Boy enjoyed the autumn countryside and listened to a stereo tape of country music. How rich could life's rewards get?

Hodge Phillips does not remember how he first noticed the disturbance in the back of the truck.

"The more I've thought about it, the more I think Big Boy called it to my attention."

In the back, one of the ordinary hunting dogs had gnawed through his rope.

"I couldn't let him jump loose and hurt himself."

So Hodge Phillips stopped his truck there on the narrow country roadway. He got out, slamming the door, and went back to retie the dog.

"The whole thing didn't take ten seconds. I just left the motor running."

Then Dog Man got back into the cab.

Or tried to.

He tugged at the door.

The door was locked.

Standing inside there, looking out with his front paws on

the window ledge, was Big Boy.

Big Boy's left front paw was squarely on the lock knob.

"He looked like he was pushing it down harder."

Phillips looked quickly to the far door.

Locked! Pushed down flat as a pancake.

All in ten seconds!

Dog Man tugged at the door handle. He was not prepared to accept this.

"You locked me out," he said to Big Boy, enunciating large syllables through the window.

Big Boy wagged his tail.

"You locked me out—now let me in!"

The ordinary dogs turned their full attention to this.

On tape, the country music singer sang away.

The truck idled through a gallon of gasoline.

How long the conversation between Dog Man and his main dog went on is not clear.

Looking through the window, Dog Man changed his appeal.

If Big Boy hadn't wanted to go hunting, he should have said something back at the house.

Did Hodge Phillips actually point at the door lock and address his main dog as "Son"?

"I called him a lot of things."

Big Boy wagged his tail.

"Once in there he had his paws up on the steering wheel." Another gallon idled away.

A fellow came along with a cotton trailer.

"I asked him to go to Dermott and get some more keys from my wife."

The man looked at the dog inside the locked cab. He said, well, all right.

Hashing over additional details would not be constructive.

The other dogs lost interest and began to cavort.

More vehicles came by.

It is no routine thing, directing traffic on a narrow country road while sitting on eight or ten cavorting dogs and ignoring that a beagle is in the cab with his paws up on the wheel, listening to music with the motor running. That's not easy if you're Dog Man.

The whole thing was over in less than an hour and a half. Half a tank of gasoline gone up in fumes.

It is not recorded what observations were made when Dog Man finally pulled up into deer camp.

Hostage Crisis Raises Quite a Stink in Booneville

It was 3:30 a.m. when a dog chorus awakened the neighborhood in Booneville.

What could such a racket be?

Clara Upton put down the details.

"My friend stepped out her front door and saw a small black dog coming toward her in the dark."

A very small dog it was, to set off such a raucous protest.

"About that time," Clara Upton says, "my friend's daughter put on the porch light."

The approaching dog turned out not to be a dog.

"It was a skunk. My friend at once turned and dashed back into her house, locked the door, and slammed the windows down."

A close call, thought the near victim.

Daylight would reveal how close.

Somebody needs to call a meeting and discuss responsibility with the neighborhood dogs.

"Come morning," says Clara Upton, "the light revealed that the skunk had settled in on the porch."

There was no getting out the front door. And the back door, it led nowhere.

Under siege, Mrs. Upton's friend got on the telephone.

"She called the sheriff and asked for help. The sheriff said sorry, he couldn't help, that she should call the City."

The victim called the City and reported that her place had been taken over by a skunk.

"The man at the City said all he could do would be to set a trap. If he could get that close. Which he might couldn't. He told my friend to call the veterinarian."

The veterinarian was thoughtful about the whole thing.

"He told my friend that all he could do would be to shoot the skunk. And of course he couldn't do that."

Why not?

"Because when he shot the skunk, the bullet might go astray. Then he would be responsible for whatever happened. If something happened."

In the meantime, you would have thought that any self-respecting dog would have run the skunk off the porch, down the street, and out of the neighborhood.

But no.

The veterinarian told Clara Upton's friend that she should call the sheriff.

She said, "I've already called the sheriff."

The veterinarian said, well, call him again.

One thing about being held captive by a skunk, you don't have to keep checking to see whether the skunk is still out there. He is out there, all right.

The victim called the sheriff again.

"The sheriff finally said, well, he guessed he could come shoot the skunk. But he couldn't take it away as it would smell up the car."

Mrs. Upton's friend said far be it from her to have the official car smelled up. Just forget she had even called.

It was getting on up in the morning.

The woman held captive by the skunk called her boss.

Clara Upton reports, "She told her boss on the telephone that she couldn't get by the porch. That she was being stopped by a skunk."

A boss does not get to be boss by accident.

A boss surges into action.

"He told my friend he would send someone to the house. A little later, here came a man carrying a garden hose. He hooked up the hose and turned the water on the skunk."

Immediately the skunk made, among other things, tracks.

"It took about fifteen dollars' worth of room spray to freshen up the porch."

There is a valuable lesson here.

"We've had a good laugh," says Clara Upton, "but the question keeps coming back. Where did the skunk go, and who would you call if it happens to somebody else?"

You'd call that somebody's boss.

Dog Owner Once a Retriever for Blackie

Ron Kinkaid does not know when the actual breaking point came.

It wasn't the second time the city of Benton picked up his dog.

It wasn't the fifth time, either.

And, no, it wasn't the tenth time Kinkaid went to the Benton pound to retrive his dog.

It wasn't even the fifteenth time.

You could say that somewhere in the neighborhood of the twentieth time Ron Kinkaid got enough.

He threw up his hands and declared to his wife, Janet, "If you want him back you'll have to go get him!"

It wasn't the five dollars' bail money.

"By then it was the humiliation," Kinkaid told us this week. "I couldn't face those people at the pound anymore."

Kinkaid is a commercial artist. About sixteen years ago he acquired a small dog, identified loosely as a cocker spaniel.

The dog was solid black. Being a creative person, Kinkaid named his dog Blackie.

A year later Kinkaid got married. This matters because if the dog authorities ever come around Kinkaid wants it understood that after fifteen years Blackie should be considered just as much his wife's dog as his own.

But with Blackie the authorities never really had to come around.

Not after the first time.

Kinkaid recalls:

"That first time he didn't come home we drove around looking and finally decided to call the pound. They had him, all right."

Benton has a leash law. The Kinkaids reported to the pound, paid the five-dollar penalty, and took Blackie home.

"Blackie never has been a lap dog or a house dog," Kinkaid says. "We told him to stay in his own yard."

The dog disappeared again. Kinkaid called the pound.

"Yes, he's here."

"Thank you. I'll be right there."

Kinkaid drove to the pound, paid the five dollars, and took his dog home. On the way he told Blackie that would be enough of that.

It wasn't nearly enough.

If the dogcatcher didn't find Blackie, Blackie found the dogcatcher.

Certain persons swear they saw the dog running to catch up with the van.

"He loved the ride," Kinkaid says. "The pound man didn't put him in the back. He just opened the door and Blackie jumped up on the front seat. That's how they went to the pound."

The time came when Kinkaid didn't even have to telephone any more. The pound called him.

"Mr. Kinkaid."

"Yes?"

"He's here again."

Accommodations at the pound were first-rate.

Kinkaid says, "Those were good people, just doing their jobs. When I got there Blackie wouldn't be out back. He'd be sitting around in the office, enjoying whatever was going on."

Kinkaid does not know how much revenue his dog has provided for the city of Benton. He does remember the five-dollar bail-out that pushed the total to ninety dollars. After that he stopped counting.

And soon after that, a few times later, that's when Kinkaid told his wife how things were going to be—"If you want him back you'll have to go get him!"

Now Blackie stays mostly on his own porch.

Some will say that because he is sixteen, and a bit overweight, he is too far along to chase dogcatchers. Maybe they are right.

But here is something.

Once Janet Kinkaid had the law laid down to her— maybe the very first time after that—when Blackie got in with the dogcatcher he was made to ride in the back of the van.

At the pound they put him out with the vagrants.

These days when the van comes by, and the pound man honks, Blackie lifts his head and mouths something uncomplimentary. And puts his head back down.

Piano-Playing Possum Wakes Up Couple

To begin with, the song could not have been written by Frederic Chopin or Fats Waller, or any piano man you've ever heard of.

Pianos were not meant to be played like that.

Was it two left hands? Or one hand and two left feet?

From where she lay on the couch, shortly after midnight, self-exiled there with a cold, Jean Parrish of Springdale could not remember ever hearing a piano played in such a manner.

Chills ran up and down her spine. And not because "Aladdin's lamp was mine."

When the "music" suddenly issued from the next room at 3300 Luvene Avenue, Jean Parrish was, in a word, terrified.

Her husband, David, is profoundly grateful to have been awakened after the concert was well under way.

"Jean had a cold. She had coughed a lot the night before."

This is David Parrish explaining why his wife was up there sleeping in the room next to the piano.

"She didn't want to disturb me with the coughing."

According to Parrish, what his wife did required remarkable courage.

"When the music started, Jean got up from the couch and forced herself to go to the door and peer into the next room.

"It was dark, but there was enough light for her to see that nobody was standing at the keyboard."

Then Jean Parrish did the remarkably courageous thing.

Holding her breath, she reached into the room, to a lamp, and flipped on the switch.

David Parrish does not remember the exact words.

He was being shaken.

It was his wife, standing over him, exhorting, "David, get up. There's a possum playing the piano."

It did not make sense. It never does when you wife shakes you in the middle of the night to say, "Ged ub. There's a bossub blaying the biano."

"Do what?"

"Ged ub!"

Parrish shook himself awake and took charge.

"Seeing the possum sitting there, on the piano keys, explained something."

The night before the possum concert, or the night before that, David and Jean Parrish thought they might have had a burglar.

"We found the VCR down on the floor, knocked off of the television set. Nothing was missing, though. A strange burglary."

The possum on the keys made sense.

"He had come in the night before, apparently through a crack in the door to the garage, and knocked the video recorder off. Obviously this possum was into entertainment."

With a flashlight, David held the piano-playing possum at bay while Jean called the Springdale police.

The call to 3300 Luvene was answered by Patrolmen Bobby Camp and Laney Morriss.

These two did not seem enthusiastic about the assignment.

"I didn't blame them," says David Parrish. It's one thing to shine a flashlight in a possum's eyes, and quite another thing to take him away from his music.

With a nightstick, one of the officers poked gently at the possum. Up until then, according to the *Springdale News,* the visiting pianist had been "grinning like Liberace."

The poked possum plumped down from the keys and went behind a couch. From there he had a police escort, tail first, out the door.

David Parrish missed most of the midnight concert.

"From what I heard, he was playing mostly Top Forty. This was a young possum."

Cat's Meow Succumbs to Dog Disaster

With a big dance revue drawing near, Mrs. Bill Sneed faced a challenge with her daughter's costume.

The costume was supposed to have a tutu. But when it arrived, the ruffle went only halfway around.

There was still time to laugh.

"This isn't a tutu," Mrs. Sneed said to her nine-year-old daughter, Jennifer. "This is a one-one."

Mrs. Sneed found a sewing lady. Together they fashioned a yellow tutu, three rows of bouncy yellow net, eighteen feet of material in all, and they attached a black ribbon. The effort was worth it. Jennifer was going to look like the cat's meow doing her tap number to "Bourbon Street."

At home, just hours before dress rehearsal, Mrs. Sneed made a jarring discovery.

She telephoned the sewing lady.

"We've got the ribbon on the wrong side!"

The sewing lady said, all right, this was no time to panic.

"If you can get it back over here we'll set the ribbon over."

Pam Sneed went to retrieve the costume, where her daughter had hung it over a doorknob. What she found removed any doubt about panic.

"The dog has eaten the tutu!"

Hearing this on the telephone, the sewing lady agreed, yes, with regard to panic, now was the time.

It is a credit to everybody that the show did, in fact, go on. Nobody in the audience could have suspected that when Jennifer got up there for her dazzling "Bourbon Street" performance, she was up there dazzling in her third tutu, or at least her second and a half.

But it was not a credit to Guthunz.

Guthunz is a sixty-four-pound Labrador retriever puppy.

Mrs. Sneed says, "From everything he'd eaten before, we thought he was a macho dog. But not a tutu!"

What the puppy has eaten in his first seven months includes two fruit trees, the carpet at the bottom of the stairs, several *Arkansas Gazettes*, and a portion of the deck attached to the house.

And now eighteen feet of yellow net, three inches wide.

"Guthunz didn't eat the ribbon," Mrs. Sneed reports. "There was just about enough of that to string him up with."

We have heard about the eating habits of Labrador retrievers. Somebody said, for example, that a ninety-pound Lab ate a car belonging to Thomas Purifoy, the executive vice president of Pulaski Bank and Trust Company.

Purifoy denied this.

"It wasn't a car. It was a Jeep station wagon. And my dog didn't eat anything but the inside back paneling."

Purifoy's dog is named Jeb. Jeb likes a good hunting trip, because he enjoys eating hunting necessities.

"He pulled a gun case through a fence and ate the gun case."

But Tom Purifoy insists that his Labrador is practically on a diet. He refers to a dog owned by Rogers Cockrill, the Little Rock lawyer.

"My dog and his are second cousins—they came from the same kennels up in Minnesota. Rogers's dog ate the whole back seat out of his Jeep."

What do you say to a Labrador retriever, after he eats the interior of a car, or a tutu?

Purifoy says you can save your breath.

"They don't hear anything you say. You just have to isolate them."

Purifoy isolated his first Labrador puppy in a back room. All furniture was removed, nothing left but some window draperies.

When the puppy got big enough to move outside, Purifoy couldn't have been prouder.

He went into the empty room and said, "There, you see. That's a good dog. He didn't eat anything."

Then they took the drapes down to start some remodeling and found that the good dog had eaten the windowsill.

This Retriever Is More Bite Than Bark

Charles Corbett of Hot Springs couldn't have been happier when he read that a Little Rock labrador retriever ate substantial portions of his master's station wagon.

Not that Corbett sells station wagons. He explains:

"Mr. Thomas Purifoy has my sympathy for the loss of whatever was eaten, but his loss is going to make my predicament easier."

Charles Corbett's predicament has been credibility.

Friends have called him a liar to his face.

Forget the friends.

His insurance company wouldn't believe him, either.

Corbett has a Labrador retriever. The dog's name is Sunset.

You have to get up early to outeat Sunset.

Corbett didn't get up early enough.

"Sunset and I camped on Island 47 at Lake Ouachita. Island 47 is out in the big middle. From Spillway Landing it's a long canoe ride by paddle, and no cinch with a small motor."

After an invigorating night spent sleeping on rocks, Corbett was awakened by robust crunching sounds.

"Sunset had got the paddle out of the canoe and was just finishing off the big end of it."

Corbett was not exactly shocked. On previous outings Sunset had eaten a poncho and most of two life preservers. The ninety-pound dog warms up on Styrofoam ice buckets.

Neither was Corbett marooned on Island 47.

"My canoe has a small motor, and I had plenty of fuel to make the long trip back."

Corbett fixed breakfast, lecturing his dog the whole time.

Sunset was stung by the criticism. After finishing his breakfast he polished off only three-fourths of what Charles Corbett had fixed for himself.

Whereupon Corbett broke camp.

Or he started to break camp.

"When I went down to begin loading I found that my dog

had eaten a hole in the front end of the canoe. The hole was down near the bottom, big enough to put your foot through."

Sunset jumped into the beached craft and stood there smiling while Corbett admired his work.

"I thought seriously about pushing the canoe out into the lake, to sink with him in it."

But the cruel urge passed?

"Nothing passed. I realized I'd lose my canoe and motor, to wet a dog that would rather swim than eat."

It took Corbett an hour to wave down two fishermen.

"I could tell they didn't like the setup. They would have taken me, but they didn't want Sunset in their boat. I told them he was a gentle dog and explained what had happened."

It did not go over big.

"You can imagine. When I told them my dog ate my boat they decided not to take either one of us."

In another hour Corbett waved down two more fishermen.

"They took us all the way to the landing. I tried to pay them but they refused."

At the landing Corbett rented a boat and motor. With Sunset sitting up front, he made the long trip back to Island 47.

"The tough thing was getting the canoe secured to the rent boat with this dog in the water trying to help me."

Corbett managed by throwing a boat cushion out into the lake a dozen times. Sunset retrieved the cushion each time, eating almost none of it.

Then the long, slow pull home, with the canoe's front end jacked up out of the water.

The whole thing didn't take more than six or seven hours.

And Sunset—did he bear up under the ordeal?

"He was so happy his teeth got sunburned."

There's a Good Reason for That Extra Pig

Somewhere south of Pine Bluff a farmer is scratching his head over how he became the mysterious owner of a well-groomed white girl pig.

The farmer has to be wondering. Well-groomed girl pigs do not fall out of the sky. Not wearing flea collars.

Her name, sir, is Bacon Bits.

She can be explained, just as Robert M. Wittig has confessed the whole thing to us.

Robert Wittig is national sales manager for Century Tube Corporation, steel post manufacturers located at the Port of Pine Bluff.

Wittig came to Arkansas a year ago, a native of Pennsylvania, graduate of the University of Scranton.

Which is to say, he has no background in pigs.

Bob and and Linda Wittig and their two young sons, Robby and Ryan, live on a five-acre place about eight miles south of Pine Bluff.

Wittig gets it off his chest:

"The boys came in one day with a hammerlock on this little thing and said, ' Look what followed us home.' "

The little thing was a white pig. Pink, actually. And in a bad way for food.

It had followed, in a hammerlock, from the edge of the woods out back.

"We went to the vet immediately, and he said, 'You've got trouble.'"

Any man who walks into a veterinarian's office carrying a pig already suspects he has trouble.

But the problem here, the vet said, was that if the pig's mother could not be found, then almost surely she would starve. No other grown lady pig would sit still for a surprise gift like that.

"So we got back into buying baby bottles," says Wittig, who last became a father four years ago. "And infant formula and vitamins."

Within two weeks the pig, named Bacon Bits, was bottle-

75

swigging a half-gallon of formula a day.

She was weaned, and relocated from her crisis quarters in the Wittig garage to a General Electric refrigerator box beside the house.

Bob Wittig discloses, "They aren't called pigs for nothing."

From baby formula, Bacon Bits got quickly into canned pet food, and then right away into the jumbo bag variety, plus watermelon rinds, cantaloupes, whatever the Wittigs would put into her large plastic feeding dish—into which the pig also put her own feet.

In eight weeks she went from three pounds to twenty-two pounds. "Twice she nearly did herself in from eating, but she got over it."

You can't have a thing like that following small boys into the house.

But Bacon Bits followed anyway. "Shoo!" Linda Wittig would say, defending the place with a broom. "You can't come in here!"—not even wearing a flea collar.

Here was, in fact, a fine pet. The pig had a pleasant disposition, was playful and acted with greater intelligence than any dog Bob Wittig could remember. But as a prospective family member, Bacon Bits had two unfortunate characteristics.

Let us discuss the other one.

Wittig says, "It's a pig's nose that gets it into trouble."

Bacon Bits rooted up the newly planted rhododendrons.

"No, no, piggy!"—Wittig scolded with a small stick.

He replanted. Bacon Bits rooted up the plant again.

"That's enough of that!" This time Wittig rapped his pig smartly on her backside.

Once again he planted. A third time Bacon Bits uprooted the rhododendrons.

On the day he had dreaded, the inevitable day, Wittig opened his car door and Bacon Bits jumped in.

"I drove miles, up and down those backroads, not feeling good about what I was doing. Then finally I saw it, a fence with a lot of pigs on the other side."

Wittig stopped and took his pig out of the car. With a mighty effort he lifted her over the fence.

"Then I just ran."

In the moving car he allowed himself a final look back.

"The other pigs were crowding up to her. Sort of a welcoming committee. Bacon Bits, she looked as happy as, well, as happy as a pig."

Children

An Uncanny Ability for Unusual Meals

The more it rained, the longer the Arkadelphia weekend got. Jason Francis, two, was cooped up in his grandmother's house.

Sick of his toys, Jason decided to get underfoot.

Grandmother Billie Taylor struggled to fix the evening meal.

She suggested, "Jason, why don't you play grocery store?"

Grocery store is played by getting all the canned goods down on the kitchen floor. You make stacks.

Jason went for it.

Maw Maw Taylor answered the telephone in the den. When she came back, Jason had sixty-two cans in stacks of various sizes.

Stacked neatly in their own pile were sixty-two labels Jason had removed from the cans.

Sixty-two silvery cans!

"Do you realize," Billie Taylor says, "what an uncanny resemblance a can of cat food has to a can of tuna fish? Shaking doesn't work, even for soup. Thumping is only for watermelons."

Of course the food had to be eaten.

"We tried opening several cans each day until a compatible menu could be devised. Soon the refrigerator was filled with covered bowls."

Finally Jason's Maw Maw and Paw Paw resolved to eat whatever got opened. No matter what!

"One night we had mackerel, tuna, salmon, and pumpkin. Paw Paw vowed he felt smarter the next day. I experienced only a strong desire to go swimming."

Drop-in dinner guests disappeared.

"My adult sons and their families had been frequent dinner guests. After this it was—'Don't know if we can come. What are we having?'"

Sauerkraut and, let's see, cherries. Yes, and Little Friskies seafood buffet.

Whatever you call it—Maw Maw's Kitchen Roulette—it failed in the worst way.

Billie Taylor encourages her grandson to take an active part in their storytelling times.

She said, "Jason, what goodies do you think were in the basket Little Red Riding Hood was taking to her grandmother?"

Jason couldn't think of anything.

Maw Maw Taylor said, "Well, what would you bring me?"

Jason looked at her and said, "Diet Coke."

"Cerelbowl": Third Time's the Charm

The Rich Luninghams of Russellville have two daughters, ages seven and two. The younger child is named Selena.

On Saturday morning Selena left watching cartoons long enough to go in and awaken her parents.

"I'm hungry and I want a cerelbowl."

That means the whole thing—bowl, spoon, cereal, milk, a complete fixup.

Selena's mother stirred just enough to mumble instructions. She told Selena that her older sister was to leave cartoons long enough to fix the cerelbowl.

How much time passed is not clear. Selena was standing at the bedside again.

"I'm hungry. She won't fix my cerelbowl."

Her mother instructed groggily but with firmness. Take the message that the cerelbowl was to be fixed right now.

It is not clear how much time went by.

On her third trip into the room the youngster appeared at her father's side of the bed. That did it.

You go tell her, Rich Luningham said, that this time was the charm—that if sister didn't get up and fix the cerelbowl then the outcome of all this would not be a pretty thing to see.

Selena started for the door, moving more rapidly than before.

She stopped, turned, and asked her father, "What's your last name?"

Child Runaways: "Back Home to Stay by Noon"

Estelle Potter, who grew up at Hot Springs, made a dramatic departure from home when she was six.

"I threatened to go all the way to the woods, which were about one block from the house."

Fifteen minutes later her mother found her still sitting on the front step.

She said, "Estelle, I thought you were leaving."

Estelle said, "I'm waiting till the woods are dark so I'll get murdered."

Her mother said, "If you're still here when your Daddy gets home from work, he'll take care of that right here in the yard."

John Workman tells about an uncle of his who ran away from home as a youngster.

The knee-britches traveler got enough of the world in a hurry and was back home in time to sit down with everybody at the supper table.

The meal progressed with nobody's speaking, until the returnee himself broke the silence:

"I see y'all still have the same old dog."

Our own problem with running away from home related to packing.

How could a departee take along the things he prized most, and still leave them behind, left around in conspicuous places as heart-breaking reminders of what a wonderful person he had been?

We never figured it out.

Linda Fulbright ran away from home twice.

The first time, at age six, she left with her doll in a paper sack and got all the way to the end of the driveway at Blytheville.

"It was a fall afternoon and I made a bed of leaves."

About 5:30 p.m., with things beginning to get dark, she

got up and went inside, deciding to give everybody another chance.

But when she left home the second time, it was forever.

Or it was supposed to be.

Mrs. Fulbright, who then lived at Arkadelphia, recalls:

"My father told me if I ever ran away, then just don't come back. But here I was seventeen years old and still being babysat by my older brother. It was too much."

While her brother talked on the telephone with his girlfriend, the aggrieved one went to her room and started packing.

She worked at it an hour, making every packing noise imaginable, slamming and unslamming a suitcase, sighing at the top of her voice.

When she left, her babysitter was still talking on the telephone.

A half-block down the street she stopped at a friend's house.

An hour later the telephone rang.

"It was my big sister. She said if I would come right then she thought she could get me back into the house."

When the wandering daughter walked in with her suitcase her father was buried so far into a newspaper only his hands were visible.

Her mother had chosen that late hour to start sewing up a storm.

So officially, the time Linda Fulbright left home forever, she never left the house.

When his daughter interrupted his Sunday afternoon nap, Max Brantley barked at her.

Martha Brantley, age four, does not cotton to being barked at.

She packed to leave home. A nightgown, a box of chalk, her Viewmaster—everything a person needs to begin a new life.

Afternoon turned to evening. There was no departure, but the atmosphere remained tense.

Not until the next morning did things lighten up.

Martha appeared and said, "Daddy, I've unpacked my Viewmaster."

The father said he was glad to hear that. He wanted to know something.

"How were you going to leave home? You're not old enough to walk across the street."

Martha had no problem with that.

"I was going to have you watch, and tell me when it was okay to cross."

Our own career as a hobo began at McGehee. Although we never made it past being a tramp.

We were five years old, and at that stage of maturity at which a person sits on books to reach his dinner plate.

Thus one develops an early appreciation for Christian teachings and the world of literature. A Bible and two Harvard Classics elevated the mouth to plate level, just right for raking in crowder peas.

Something rotten happened and we announced that we were leaving home.

Whoever this was supposed to have crushed held the door open, facilitating our departure.

No need trying to stop us. We were at the end of our road.

That didn't sound right, so we changed it to the end of our "row."

That didn't sound right, either. On the third goodbye we made it "roast."

To this day we do not know what a person reaches the end of just before leaving home.

"You're letting flies in."

Ignoring that pleading, we set out on life's highway.

Fifty feet from the house, weary from travel, we sat down to rest beneath a tree and sort through our equipment.

It does not take long to sort through two matches. We struck one and saved the other for a rainy day.

Several months passed, although the sun never went down or came up. If we could have told time, it probably was more like forty-five minutes.

And getting close to supper.

We got up and walked to the house, going around back in the manner of a true hobo.

No longer being a resident there, we knocked at the door and retreated into the yard.

The man who had formerly been our father appeared and looked down through the screen.

"Yes?"

We told him we had come for a Bible.

"A Bible?" He put a hand thoughtfully over his mouth. Behind him some crowder peas were cooking.

"Did you want to read it or sit on it?"

We decided to go in and sit on it.

Youth Discovers Hazards of Friday Night Television

In the aftershock the details are hazy.

Beverly Jones remembers that she was walking down the hallway of her home in Mena.

Mrs. Jones's husband had not yet come in from work. Her older son was away with a youth group.

So that left Beverly Jones and her ten-year-old son, Kyle, there at home on a quiet Friday evening.

"I was walking down the hall when it happened. This terrific explosion."

An explosion that rattled the house.

Followed immediately by an eerie hissing noise.

Stunned, Beverly Jones started running toward the room where she knew her son was watching television.

That was the direction of the blast.

Everybody knows what a no-account thing J.D. Hogg is.

Boss Hogg. He gets on there every Friday night, on "The Dukes of Hazzard," and makes life miserable for the Duke boys.

Boss Hogg and his chocolate-covered barbecue.

And his hatful of whipped cream.

It is about more than a person can take.

Do not ask the young man, himself, what happened.

Beverly Jones's son, Kyle, was sitting there as always on Friday night, in the rocking chair, seven feet from the color television screen.

This night there was one difference.

The fifth-grader, having the house practically to himself, had gotten out his older brother's pellet gun.

Sitting down to watch "The Dukes of Hazzard," Kyle had that weapon in his lap.

When Beverly Jones hurried into the explosion room she experienced a feeling of vast relief.

Her son appeared to be all right.

Except for an indescribable expression on his face.

"I can't begin to say what he looked like," says the mother. "Kyle is such an easy-going person."

Boss Hogg had gone too far. In the face of dirty dealings that no friend of the Duke boys could abide, Kyle leaned forward in the rocking chair, drew down and squeezed the trigger of the pellet gun.

Beverly Jones looked from her son to see smoke pouring out through a hole in the television screen. The last of the eerie hissing.

In the rocking chair, the boy regarded the gun in his hands as some alien object.

Ordinarily Kyle gets up early on Saturday morning to watch cartoons, keeping the sound turned down while the rest of the household sleeps.

On the Saturday morning after Boss J.D. Hogg was blown away, Beverly and David Jones got up hearing no sounds at all.

There was another television set. But after eight o'clock Kyle still was in his room.

"His dad hadn't come in early enough the night before for them to have their talk," Mrs. Jones says. "Kyle went to his room early. I worried about his reaction to what he had done. Once I went in there and he was sitting in the middle of his room with his knife in front of him. But the knife wasn't open."

Kyle is buying a color picture tube.

His mother called around. The tube will cost up there in the hundreds.

So far, Kyle has saved up almost seven dollars.

He is elated.

"Saturday was great for him," his mother says. "He finally got up and had the talk with his dad. Then he went around being happy all day, just knowing he wasn't a dead person."

The picture tube?

"Oh, he's sure it will take all his life to pay for it."

Maybe not.

We have discussed this incident with several fathers, each

of whom hears Boss Hogg going at it somewhere in the house every Friday night.

One of the fathers said, "This Kyle fellow in Mena. Do you suppose he's ever heard of 'This Gun's for Hire'?"

"It's Not Nice to Fool Mother Nature"

Mrs. Robert Underwood of Arkadelphia spent a month recently with her daughter's family at St. Louis.

The long visit was altogether pleasant, with one recurring exception.

Three Monday mornings in a row Mrs. Underwood's grandson, a first-grader named Timothy, showed up at breakfast with a fiery red throat.

The youngster had no fever, but the decision was to keep him home from school. That was the first two Mondays.

Each time Timothy seemed to make a nice recovery around nine o'clock in the morning.

Grandma Underwood thought it odd that these hit-and-run sore throats hit and ran only on Monday.

Something else was peculiar, too.

Every Monday when Timothy opened his mouth and said "Ahhh" Mrs. Underwood was reminded of some nickel-a-quart perfume she bought as a little girl.

That third Monday morning, after the throat examination, she followed the stricken young scholar back to his room.

Mrs. Underwood said, "You want to share with me?"

"Share what, Grandma?"

"Whatever it is you've been drinking."

Timothy said he didn't drink anything—"You just put the powder in your mouth and it melts."

Strawberry Kool-aid.

It turned out that Monday was Timothy's turn to stand up in front of the class and sing "Good Morning, Bluebirds."

He made it in time to sing that day.

We knew a young scholar who, back when he attended Woodruff Elementary School, suffered frightful Monday morning fever attacks.

"Hurry! Feel my head!" He said that while staggering red-faced out of his room.

The heat would sear a parent's palm.

Mercifully, it passed as fast as it came.

It passed too fast.

To keep his fever built up, the student ran repeatedly back to his room, to put his face next to a wall heater.

His malady was diagnosed, and cured for all time, the Monday morning he ran in there and stood too close, burning the grating pattern into his forehead.

From Lake Hamilton, Honey Mitchell recalls being hit by a fever attack on Children's Day at church.

The medical reason was never discovered.

But Honey Mitchell knew what was wrong.

"They always made me do the most cornball things. I felt like a fool.

"When I was six I had to carry a flag on the stage with four daisies. I had to point out what each daisy stood for. I remember I had to say, 'The third one stands for my teacher true, and I tell you she's a daisy, too.'

"Now I didn't think of my teacher as a daisy. More like a bitterweed. She had an overbite and wore gold-rimmed glasses. She would brook no nonsense. There was no fun in our work with her.

"I rebelled. I said I will not call that old mean goober-toothed woman no daisy. I won't wave a flag and act silly. And I won't wear a dress that feels like pie crust. That was organdy. I wonder if kids still wear organdy.

"My mother took me out behind the church and beat my back end until—well, I got up on that stage and waved my daisy flag and made a horse's tail out of myself.

"When the second Sunday in May dawned I didn't wear pie crust or wave a flag. I had fever. Not just a paltry amount of fever, but a high fever. The doctor could find nothing wrong.

"I've never cared for daisies. And I never hit one of my kids, even in self-defense."

This Test Has Only One Question

Nancy Foshe of Mountain Home tells us a story about four high school youths who skipped school.

Shortly after lunch the four got crimpy and made it to class, explaining that they had a flat tire.

The teacher swallowed the story. At least she appeared to. She smiled and said, "You boys missed a test this morning."

On instructions, the youths took widely separated seats and got out pencils and paper.

"The test has just one question," the teacher said. "Which tire was flat?"

Personally we never favored that approach to education. It makes young scholars skeptical of the system and inhibits creative growth.

As a young scholar we once telephoned the office at Little Rock Senior High School to explain to Miss Ernestine Opie that we were at home, sick in bed.

Miss Opie said, "I'd be sick too if I had cars driving through my bedroom."

Ma'am?

"It sounds like you live in a phone booth."

We experienced a loud coughing attack.

Miss Opie said, "Describe your symptoms."

We explained that in addition to our high fever and nausea, the split vision resulting from loss of blood seemed to have left one leg shorter than the other.

Miss Opie said she was sorry to hear all this.

"Will you be back in school tomorrow?"

We said, oh yes ma'am, we'd be there tomorrow.

Miss Opie said, after a slight pause, "I'll tell you what, young man. You know where this school building is. I want to hear those corduroy britches sing when they come through the front door."

They were singing before she hung up.

Miss Edna Middlebrook, when she was our twelfth-grade homeroom teacher, announced near the end of the spring semester that a member of the class had been skipping gym.

Miss Middlebrook said she had heard this indirectly from Coach Wilson Matthews and that it was just about more than she could take.

It was nothing of the sort. She could take anything and dish out twice that much.

But on this day in the spring Miss Middlebrook had her homeroom scholars in front of her and she was saying what a rotten shame it was for a senior in high school—a twelfth-grader!—to jeopardize his entire scholastic career by not doing his simple duty of going to gym class, but instead pursuing the gutless course of slipping over to Ponder's Drug Store across the street and smoking cigarettes.

The classroom was engulfed by a deathly stillness.

Miss Edna said sharply:

"I don't have to call your name. You know who you are. Will the individual who's been skipping gym march out of here right now and report to Coach Matthews!"

Four individuals stumbled toward the door. We would have too except that, mercifully, one knee was bouncing so wildly out of control we couldn't stand up.

Miss Middlebrook stood there, arms folded, serene, her expression belonging on Mount Rushmore.

"You four get back to your seats. The rest of the class is dismissed."

We saw them minutes later, she leading the way down the hall, the four who had betrayed themselves following along as though in chains.

Edna Middlebrook and Ernestine Opie, who knew what kind of creative growth to inhibit, have been gone awhile. They're up there straightening halos.

Red Faces

Pryor Shows Diplomacy, Delicacy in Handling Laundry

A woman in Baxter County is persuaded that nobody has a touch more delicate than U.S. Senator David Pryor.

The word comes from a reader who asks to keep her sister's name a secret.

"This lady was driving away from the coin laundry in Mountain Home when she rode around the corner and saw Senator Pryor crossing the street. Naturally she slowed down as he came across to shake her hand."

The handshake was deferred for a brief moment.

"Before reaching in the car window to greet her, the senator deftly retrieved something from the hood of her car."

Without a hint of embarrassment, Senator Pryor said, "I believe you've lost part of your laundry."

He handed through two pairs of women's underthings.

It is human nature to wonder what that woman had to say, reunited in such a manner with her unmentionable clothing.

Was it something with a blush?

"Why, Senator—well, that is, thank you very much."

Something political?

"Thanks, Senator. Tippecanoe and Pryor too."

According to her sister, what this woman said to Senator Pryor, as she retook possession of her garments, was, "Oh, my! I've really got something to tell my grandchildren!"

"Tie" Exchange Brings Pink to his Cheeks

For his birthday H.L. (Hank) Lindsey of Fort Smith got identical neckties.

The ties were blue with a gray stripe, from the same store.

Lindsey returned one of the ties to the store. Or that's what he meant to do.

The sales clerk acquired a perplexed expression.

She said, looking into the sack, "Sir, is there something wrong with this?"

Hank Lindsey said oh no. "I love it," he said. "It's just that I have another one like it."

The clerk reddened. "You're returning this because you already have one?"

Lindsey said, "Right. And I'm not returning it. I just want to exchange it for something that will go better with brown."

The clerk took a step and a half backward. "All right, if you'll pick it out yourself, I'll return this to stock."

She returned the merchandise to stock, all right—to brassieres. The man who already had one like it, and loved it, hurried after her, reacquired his item, and left with no further word.

Cheryl Lindsey will exchange her husband's tie.

"Idiot" Finally Finds "Blabbermouth" at End of Line

After what seemed like the fiftieth busy signal, A.R. (Doc) McCurdy of Hot Springs threw up his hands and dialed the operator.

"Would you see if a phone has been left off the hook?"

The operator reported back that the telephone in question was in use.

It flabbergasted Doc McCurdy.

"How long can one blabbermouth idiot talk?"

Marie McCurdy mumbled a non-reply to her husband.

"After a while I was aware that Doc was trying to call again, and that he was beginning to fume."

Mrs. McCurdy spoke consolingly. "Honey, what number are you trying to reach?"

Doc fumed, "I'm trying to reach six...two...four"—in sharply punctuated syllables he gave the number.

Marie McCurdy asked, "Did you say six...two...four"—in sharply punctuated syllables she repeated it.

Doc said, "Yes!"

Marie said, "That's *our* number!"

Doc McCurdy went outside to walk things off.

When he came back in, Marie McCurdy said, "Honey, can I ask you a question?"

Under control again, Doc said, "Certainly."

Marie said, "How long *can* one blabbermouth idiot talk on the telephone?"

Doc went back outside to walk things off agin.

Mrs. McCurdy says, "The whole thing has passed."

Except for one thing.

"Doc can't remember who he wanted to call in the first place."

Balloon Lets Missourian Get Wind of Name, Number

Among the presents at Dorothy McGuire's birthday party, back on August 28, was a cluster of helium balloons.

Mrs. McGuire does not recall how old the birthday made her.

"I'm up there." She recalls that much.

The birthday balloons were fun. For a week after the party they adorned the apartment at Lakewood House in North Little Rock.

Then the balloons began to get puckery. They seemed to be going fast.

What Dorothy McGuire did, she cannot explain.

"Don't ask me why I did it because I don't know."

What she did was, she selected a puckery silver balloon from the cluster.

With a felt-tipped marker, navy blue, she wrote her name on the silver balloon.

Her name and telephone number.

And not "Dorothy" McGuire, either.

She made it "Dot" McGuire.

Don't ask why she did that.

From her patio on the second floor of Lakewood House, Mrs. McGuire launched her birthday balloon.

Launched is hardly the word.

"The balloon whizzled around, then settled straight to the ground."

That sight was deflating. Also disturbing.

"I wasn't about to let anybody around here find the balloon with my name and telephone number. Not with 'Dot' on it."

Mrs. McGuire hurried downstairs to retrieve the puckery balloon and finish its destruction.

The birthday balloon was gone.

It was in the early evening, about 6:30. The voice on the telephone was alive with enthusiasm.

The voice belonged to a teenager.

He was looking for "Dot."

Dorothy McGuire's birthday balloon had disappeared so long ago, weeks ago, she had even stopped worrying about it.

"Where are you?" the enthusiastic caller asked.

Mrs. McGuire replied, "I'm in North Little Rock, Arkansas."

The caller exclaimed, "Oh, wow!"—or the equivalent of that.

He had been calling all over.

"I found your balloon, Dot. You didn't put your area code on the phone number."

"Dot" McGuire experienced a sinking feeling.

"Where are you calling from?" she asked.

The excited young man said, "I'm north of West Plains, Missouri." The tone of his voice added, "Baby."

Was it the wind?

Was it Fate?

Was it Southwestern Bell?

Something unseen plucked Dorothy McGuire's puckery telephone number from the ground in North Little Rock and delivered it weeks later into the eager hands of a young man hundreds of miles to the north.

She said to her caller, "Honey, you shouldn't talk any longer. We're running up your telephone bill."

Mrs. McGuire sensed uncertainty settling in north of West Plains, Missouri.

She said, "That balloon you found. It was from a birthday party given for me by my daughter."

Whatever the young man said, hanging up, it was the equivalent of, "Oh, wow!"

Message in Bottle Endures Ravages of Water, Time

On the morning of October 6, a Thursday, Kevin Carson launched his bottle from the Main Street Bridge in Little Rock.

Sealed inside, against the ravages of water and time, was Carson's message to an unknown kindred soul.

Catch the spirit of this thing:

"Hello. My name is Kevin Carson. I am 22 years old, a mechanical engineer at a high-rise hotel in Little Rock, Arkansas, in the United States. I dropped this bottle in the Arkansas River from the Main Street Bridge in Little Rock, Arkansas, on October 6, 1983. The purpose was to see how far it would travel before someone found it. I ask whoever has found this bottle to please write or notify me in some way as to who found it, the date found, and where it was found. Here is my address: Kevin Carson, 4611 Stratton Avenue, Little Rock, Arkansas, U.S.A. 72209."

One recalls the words of the great English sea captain, James Cook, who wrote of his voyage of discovery, "I had ambition to go not only farther than any man had gone, but to go as far as it was possible to go."

At the last minute, Kevin Carson put in his business card. He sealed the bottle with silicone, an engineer's trick.

The hour of launch was 10:30 a.m.

For a long moment he watched the bottle on the water's surface.

He had said to his wife, Monda, "I wonder how far it will go?"

Down the Arkansas to the Mississippi? Down the Mississippi to the Gulf? Across what oceans? Through what caverns measureless to man? To wash up on what alien shore?

Kevin Carson wondered how old he would be when his message was found. At age twenty-two, would he live to know it?

He walked back to work at the Executive Inn.

Because the day was lovely, Rodgers Critz decided to have

lunch in the park by the river. Rodgers Critz and about twenty others from the firm of Cromwell Truemper Levy Parker and Woodsmall, architects and engineers.

At noon the group walked down to the park to eat.

Rodgers Critz wandered away.

"I just went walking. Went up to see the little rock. Then wandered back."

As Critz returned, the others were looking toward something down at the water's edge. A group staring exercise.

"There's a bottle down there," somebody said to Critz.

"It looks like there's a note in it," somebody else said.

Rodgers Critz wondered why nobody had gone down to investigate. He went.

"What is it?" they shouted as he reached the bottle.

"It's a bottle with a note in it."

"What does it say?"

Critz could not tell. Picking the bottle up, he found it tightly sealed.

"I can't get it open."

Who had set this bottle adrift? From what distant shore? For what reason? The answers were sealed inside.

Rodgers Critz threw the bottle down on a rock, an architect's and engineer's trick.

"What does it say?" the group shouted from above.

Critz sorted through the broken glass for the note, finding also a business card.

"Read it!" the group shouted.

Critz unfolded the note, held it up, and read to those above him on the riverbank:

"Hello. My name is Kevin Carson. I am 22 years old, a mechanical engineer at a high-rise..."

At 1:30 p.m. on Thursday, October 6, Kevin got a telephone message left by a man who purportedly had found his message in a bottle washed ashore at Vicksburg, Mississippi.

From Little Rock to Vicksburg in three hours. Some current!

In the words of Rodgers Critz, there are some "wits" in the Cromwell firm.

"We have some Orientals in our bunch. I didn't even want

to think about what somebody might find that afternoon in Japan."

Critz was appalled by his own part in the adventure.

He wrote to Kevin Carson, "I'm sorry I couldn't throw your bottle back into the river. I had to break it to find out what to do."

Following instructions, Critz advised Carson of the time and location of the bottle's recovery: "Found in Arkansas River—Noon, Oct. 6, 1983."

Place of recovery: "One block west of the Main Street Bridge."

That's upstream.

Reach Out and Dial a Daddy

This is an apology of sorts to a nice gentleman up in Siloam Springs. After ten days he might still be sitting by the telephone, waiting for a call that isn't going to come.

Our girl Sally Kirby feels rotten about her part in the thing.

When the bad winds hit two Friday nights ago Kirby telephoned her father in Siloam Springs. Direct-dialed him, as we say.

"Daddy?"

"Yes."

"How are you?"

"I'm fine. How are you?"

"I'm fine. Did you make it through the wind?"

"Yes, we're all right. How about you?"

As she was talking, Sally Kirby was cooking, dragging the telephone around the kitchen, stirring, putting lids on.

"Daddy, you sound like you've got a head cold."

Daddy had one, all right, but he was bearing up. "Oh, yes, I've been working out in the yard. You know how it is with all this stuff in the air."

But it was more than the head cold.

The nice man's voice—"This isn't my Daddy," Kirby thought. She stopped cooking and started thinking.

They had another round of "Fine, thanks" and "Not much" and "So are we."

Kirby says, getting red in the face telling about it, "The conversation was just too pleasant, it had gone on too long, I couldn't come out and tell him the whole thing was a big mistake."

So?

"So I just lied."

Kirby told the man on the telephone, "Listen, Daddy, somebody's at the door. I'll have to go, and I'll call you back."

Daddy said fine, and was gone.

After she hung up, Kirby walked around, her arms folded, feeling ashamed about the whole thing, her interest in cooking gone.

She made another telephone call to Siloam Springs, this

time dialing carefully.

"Daddy?"

"Yes. Hi there. How are you?"

"Daddy, we didn't talk earlier tonight, did we?"

The answer was what Kirby knew it would be.

"My real Daddy said, no, we hadn't talked. He was watching something on television, so we went on and had about the same conversation I'd had with the other Daddy."

It Takes a Heap o' Heaping to Make Cookie Crumble

When our friend Reid opened his fortune cookie at the Hong Kong Restaurant he read:

"Signifies a favor or kindness from some you realize."

Mrs. Reid asked, "What does yours say?"

Reid stalled, "I got some soy sauce on it."

When Mrs. Reid went to powder her nose, he picked up his fortune and read it again:

"Signifies a favor or kindness from some you realize."

Reid could not make himself understand what this meant. There was no beginning or end. Quite possibly no middle.

He considered demanding another fortune cookie. But at the Hong Kong cash register May Jeu was chatting with other customers. And in the back—Reid stood up and looked through the window into the kitchen—back there Jack Jeu was going about his procedures.

With a cleaver in his hand, Jack Jeu is six-feet-nine and weighs four hundred pounds. He could take James Bond any time.

Reid sat down and sneaked a look at his wife's fortune.

It advised, "Attend to business."

Then for a third time Reid puzzled over his own fortune.

It is not easy to know what the cookies have in store for us.

Our best guess, we told Reid when he showed us the small white strip of paper—there was no soy sauce on it—our best guess was that his fortune was written by the same person who wrote the instructions for Irene Wassell's new hair curler.

Mrs. Wassell bought an electric wand of some sort. The instructions that came with it, things not to do while operating the wand, were as long as the cord.

One thing not to do was, "Do not plug in while falling into bathtub full of water." It was something like that.

Another instruction was, "Do not approximate curler to head while being in sleep."

In other words, we reminded Reid, instructions written in other lands, and cookies written as well, might not mean the same thing to the author as to the person falling into the bathtub.

Crossing oceans, languages undergo subtle changes.

He could forget about taking this up with Jack Jeu. The other land Jack Jeu came from was Desha County, down in southeast Arkansas. We have known Jack since he was a little boy. At that time he was only six-feet-four and weighed 250 pounds.

But Reid was not content.

"The way I see it," our friend said, "a fortune cookie ought to tell you something about the future. Unlock a mystery."

If it didn't predict something, then the cookie at least should say something inspirational.

He quoted an example.

"It takes a heap o' heaping to make a heap o' heap."

Reid did not make up that inspirational saying.

"It was said originally by Edgar A. Guest. Or maybe Paul Harvey."

Whichever, after reading something like that a man could walk out of the Hong Kong thinking large thoughts.

Unless the Hong Kong was in Hong Kong. In which case he would demand another fortune cookie.

It's true that fortune cookies have come to lack something in the way of excitement.

Imagine a customer's reaction if he fumbled through the crumbs and pulled out a small white slip of paper saying, "The egg rolls were on the house."

This is merely a thought. Certainly not something we are suggesting to the proprietors of the Hong Kong Restaurant.

Or the cookie might reveal, "That old friend who just dropped by the table and you introduced him to your wife as Fred. His name was Dave."

Or, "You won't make any sense out of this fortune cookie because you've had three rice wines too many."

Or, *"Signifies a favor or kindness from some you realize"* means "Young thugs out on the parking lot are making off with your hubcaps."

"I Love You and Can't Remember Your Name"

At the grocery store Mrs. Thomas DeLong spotted at the far end of an aisle a woman she had known all her life, but whose name—so help her Hannah!—just faded into thin air.

Mrs. DeLong swerved her buggy to another aisle, to get her thoughts in order.

She described it later:

"It was the most ridiculous feeling. I knew that woman as well as I knew myself."

For a person nearing maturity, this is nothing to be ashamed of.

We sat down in the car the other day and looked at the keys for five minutes, trying to remember what to do first.

Suddenly the other woman rounded the far end of the new aisle, pushing her buggy, engrossed in shopping.

Again Sarah DeLong retreated, desperate now in the conviction that the woman was a relative.

She hated herself for being in the same store.

Two more peelbacks later, having run out of aisles, the women confronted each other at six buggy lengths.

Their eyes met for the first time.

The other woman smiled broadly, reddened and started forward, one hand extended and the other hand over her mouth.

"I'm Mildred Tillis, and I've been feeling like such a fool because I love you, and I can't remember your name."

Two old neighbors from Jonesboro met for the first time in twenty years.

Once they stopped running from each other.

But that problem can be solved in laughter, as it was with Sarah DeLong and Mildred Tillis, and a store employee who overheard and joined in the laughter himself.

The problem is not what to say to somebody you meet in the grocery store for the first time in twenty years.

The real problem is what to say to somebody you meet in the grocery store the second and third times on the same shopping trip.

And the fourth time.

And so on around the store.

It begins at the buggies.

"Hello there! Doing the chores?"

"Absolutely—got to eat! How's the family?"

"Family's fine. Good to see you."

"Good to see you, too."

The old acquaintances push away in different directions and meet minutes later at the coffee grinder.

"Fancy seeing you here!"

"Yeah—haven't we met somewhere before?"

By actual count eight heh!-heh!s are exchanged.

"You go ahead and grind."

"No, no, you go ahead. I'll just stand here and go over my list."

At the cottage cheese, five minutes later, the count escalates to fourteen heh!-heh!s.

Apiece.

"Listen, we've got to stop meeting like this."

"You bet—people are going to talk!"

Ensues a serious discussion of small curd over large, both being improved if you reach toward the back and get a carton with a later date on it.

"And how's the family?"

"They're still fine."

At the coconuts there are no heh!-heh!s. Only tight smiles.

"Don't tell me you're going to get a coconut?"

"I was going to, but now I don't know. Are you going to get a coconut?"

"I wasn't going to, but now I might."

It is agreed that although the price is too high, now is a good time to buy a coconut. Unless one decided otherwise.

"It's good to see you."

"You bet. See you around."

Seeing them together, two minutes later in the checkout line, you would take them for perfect strangers.

Recalling Old Friend Difficult When You've Just Met

At the farmers' market in Little Rock early Tuesday, Wanda Sifers of Redfield ran into a dear old friend whose name she couldn't remember.

"Hello, there," Mrs. Sifers said, hugging her dear old friend's neck.

"Well, hello," the dear old friend said.

Wanda Sifers rushed ahead, confident the name would come.

"How are all the folks?" she asked.

The folks couldn't have been better.

Nothing happened, so Wanda Wifers shifted mental gears.

"I don't think I've seen you since the twins were born"— she dug into her purse and produced a snapshot of her twin granddaughters.

The dear old friend said, my, what twins—"I know you're proud of them."

Mrs. Sifers said, "That's Shawna on the left and Sandra on the right."

The dear old friend said, "My!"

It just wasn't working. Wanda Sifers was beginning not to like herself, and the dear old friend's expression grew more remote by the second.

The Redfield resident came right out with it.

"This is so ridiculous. For the life of me, I can't remember your name."

It wasn't ridiculous to the dear old friend.

"We've never met," she said. "I'm the one who shouted at you over there at the stoplight to ask how to get on the parking lot."

It turned out that Wanda Sifers's dear old friend was from Brainerd, Minnesota. She was visiting friends in Arkansas, and had an interest in grits.

Mrs. Sifers opined that grits were more to be talked about.

The visitor from Minnesota suspected as much.

She said, "My brother was in the Army here. He came back to Brainerd raving about something you do with a mixture of molasses and grits."

Wanda Sifers of Redfield told what she would do with a mixture of molasses and grits.

The visitor said, "I thought so. My brother is a big bull shooter. But he loved Arkansas, and I guess he was just telling us about the friendliness of the people down here."

Well, she had her own proof of that.

"I haven't even had breakfast yet, and already I've been hugged by a perfect stranger and seen a picture of the babies."

On Being Temporarily Bested by Inevitable Fallback

Pat Best goes to the beauty shop early, at 7:00 a.m. With fall and its time change coming up, she asked the beauty shop for a new appointment time.

"I don't want to be getting here in the dark," Mrs. Best explained.

The beauty shop scheduler did not understand the request.

"Actually, Pat, when you come at seven o'clock next week, it will be later."

Mrs. Best is a civilized person.

"Spring forward, fall back," she reminded the scheduler, demonstrating with gentle hand movements.

The scheduler smiled and nodded.

"That's right. It means that when you get here next time it will be an hour after seven."

Mrs. Best is a patient person. But she is no fool.

"Are you trying to tell me that if I set my clock back, and start getting up an hour earlier in the morning—are you standing there and telling me it's going to be lighter outside?"

The beauty shop scheduler consulted her appointment calendar. She said, "What time would you like to come in?"

That was only the beginning of the Standard Time conspiracy against Pat Best.

"I went home and told Eddie what they said at the beauty shop."

Eddie is Mrs. Best's husband, Eddie Best, a Little Rock advertising executive.

"He took their side," Pat Best said, her lip trembling.

It really hurt. The Bests have grown sons. They've come a long way together.

"Why do you suppose he wants to get me out of the house while it's still dark?"

Eddie Best had a long explanation about the conversion to Standard Time. He sat Mrs. Best down and brought coffee to her.

"Once it seemed to be making sense, what he was saying. But then it went away, before my very eyes."

What her husband explained to Mrs. Best was this:

"When we set our clock back an hour and get up and six, it will be what used to be seven. So even though we put the clock back to five, you'll be getting to the beauty shop at eight."

Or that's what she thought he said.

We advised Mrs. Best to see a lawyer.

"Eddie's right! I can see it now."

This time she was under control, Pat Best was, her lips more or less not trembling.

There were still two days until Standard Time.

"Do you see these clocks?"

Mrs. Best had no clocks. She was holding up her hands, forming circles with thumbs and forefingers.

We admired the clocks.

She said, "Let's say that both of these clocks are set at six o'clock. Let's say we set this one back to five o'clock"—she shook the "clock" in her left hand—"so that when the alarm goes off, it's not the same time it used to be. It's actually"—a glaze passed over Mrs. Best's eyes.

We tried to sit her down, bring some coffee to her.

She threw the clocks down and ran out of the office.

It is a pleasure to report that whenever dawn breaks this morning, at whatever new hour, Mr. and Mrs. Best still will be in the same time zone.

"I don't know how I could have been so dumb," Mrs. Best told us, her eyes sparkling.

She had a piece of paper in her hand.

"When you look at it this way, it just jumps right out at you."

Mrs. Best showed us the formula for understanding conversion to Standard Time. On paper she had written:

"5:00—6:00

"6:00—7:00

"7:00—8:00"

Had her husband given this formula to her?

"Oh, my, no! He's sick of talking about it. I figured the whole thing out myself."

Olden Days

When Someone Thought of Counting the Eggs

A friend was lamenting the passing of the neighborhood grocery store.

"There must be a few left," he said, "but I can't imagine where they are."

Not the modern convenience stores, with totem-pole fronts and lucky number names. He shrugged these off.

"They seem to get held up every fifteen minutes, but I can't get very excited about that. Every time I come out of one of those stores I feel like I've been robbed myself."

He missed his old neighborhood grocery store.

He remembered his mother's saying, "Calvin, go to Mr. Doster's and get me some eggs."

Mr. Doster. Not Mr. Savabundle.

Calvin walked the two blocks to Doster's, barefooted in the summertime, and made the bell jangle when he opened the front screen door.

"Hi, Miz Doster."

"Hi, Calvin."

"It sure it hot, isn't it?"

"It sure is, Calvin."

But it wasn't. Not to a nine-year-old boy. The fan whomped circles of air down on Mrs. Doster's head, lifting the top sheet on her grocery order pad, showing the carbon underneath.

Mrs. Doster took grocery orders on the telephone. Her older son, Pinky Doster, filled the orders in delivery boxes. Her younger son, Little Pink, delivered the boxes on his bicycle.

Mr. Doster, himself, kept to the back with the meat, rearranging the baloney and spiced ham and the hoop cheese. On Friday afternoons he went out behind the store and strangled a lot of chickens.

"Miz Doster, when you get through with that piece of carbon paper, what are you going to do with it?"

Calvin was eye-level with the countertop. He stuck his chin up there, resting it on the backs of his hands.

Mrs. Doster said, oh, the carbon paper usually got worn out from so much writing on it. She was working on an order and did not look up. Mrs. Doster had a sweat mustache and although she was very old, probably close to forty, Calvin thought she was beautiful.

"What can I do for you, Calvin?"

"Mama wants some eggs."

Mrs. Doster reached beneath the counter and pulled out a paper sack, which she popped open in a professional manner, and then handed the sack across the counter. "You know where they are?"

Calvin said, "Sure."

He took the sack and walked down the counter, passing a jar of corn candy, and another one of red hots, and another filled with hard banana candy, each piece wrapped up. He passed a cigar box, opened and piled up with ration stamps for sugar and coffee and meat.

At the red Coca-Cola box Calvin lifted one end of the hinged lid. Murking down there in the icy slush were big grape drinks and orange and strawberries and RC Colas. The only person Calvin ever saw drink a small Coke was Mrs. Doster.

He fished out a piece of ice, wiped it on his pants, and put the ice in his mouth, being careful not to get the egg sack wet.

At a big wire basket near the back of the store Calvin counted out his eggs and said "Hi" to Mr. Doster, who had on his apron and was talking with a meat truck driver.

Going out, Calvin passed the front counter.

"Did you get a dozen?" Mrs. Doster asked.

Calvin said, "Yes'm. You want to count 'em?" He unrolled the sack top and held it open.

Mrs. Doster said, "No, I don't want to count the eggs." She took the slip of carbon paper from her order book and dropped it in on top of the eggs.

That was a long time ago.

Our friend remembered that before he got old enough to leave home Mr. Doster died. Mrs. Doster got married again not long after that, and she and Little Pink moved away with the new Mr. Doster.

The store hasn't been there for many years.

The way things have been pushed around, he wasn't even sure he could find the neighborhood.

A Feast at Your Neighborhood Grocery

Jeffrey Claussen of North Little Rock says that recent recollections here about old-time neighborhood grocery stores did not do justice to the institution.

Especially at mealtime.

Claussen says:

"During more than twenty years of military service I ate in high-toned establishments around much of the world, but the last time I truly 'dined' away from home was on crackers and cheese, sitting on an empty orange crate in our neighborhood grocery store on Washington Avenue in North Little Rock. A pint of cold milk from a glass bottle and some fig newtons completed this feast."

Claussen swears he would give a month's retirement pay to enjoy such a meal again, on the condition that he'd be joined on the next orange crate by an old man who used to come to the store and eat sardines because his wife wouldn't let him eat them at home.

Paul Meers remembers some crackers and cheese he ate at a small grocery store in Lonoke County.

Meers and his hunting partner, Sid Rucker, had been on a Christmas Eve quail hunt, walking the fields most of the day, getting cold and hungry. Heading home, they stopped at the store at Kerr's Station.

"We were in the store there eating crackers and cheese and warming up when this little old woman came in. Her clothes were not adequate for the weather and she was work-worn. I remember especially how rough her hands looked. She opened up one of them and there was a quarter in her palm."

The woman told the storekeeper that she was going to buy a Christmas present for her husband.

Paul Meers recalls:

"She put her face up to that glass showcase, right up against it, and one by one picked out five presents. I believe the first was the peppermint stick, and a five-cent peppermint stick went a long way in those days. Then she picked out a red bandana handkerchief. Next was a corncob pipe—she said her husband would like that—and to go with the pipe she got a sack of tobacco."

Meers cannot remember what the fifth present was. He thinks it might have been a jew's-harp. But what a face on that woman! It was hard to watch her, shopping, and swallow crackers and cheese.

Meers said to Sid Rucker, when they were back in the car, and on the last leg home at twilight:

"You know, a lot of men whose wives can spend one hundred dollars on their Christmas presents would give anything to see the love we saw on that woman's face."

We had a rampant envy for folks who owned neighborhood grocery stores. What lavish lives they must have led!

Mrs. E.L. Alexander recalls how lavish some of it was. Her family operated a home-owned grocery store at Seventh and Pine Streets. Now they drive near there on the Wilbur Mills Freeway and look down and remember.

"One thing we remember was the way the perishables reached the family table—*just* before they perished. One of the most memorable of these is the banana pudding."

As a store family, the Alexanders couldn't figure out when to eat lunch.

"Business seemed to pick up about the time we sat down. One day when the 'ripest' bananas had been salvaged for a pudding and the family was seated at the table, the late noon rush began, keeping both my husband and me busy in the store while the children ate alone.

"Their lunch was over about the time our rush was over and as our four-year-old son climbed from his chair and ascended the stairs for the afternoon nap he called to me, 'Mother, the pudding is good, even if you did use rotten bananas.'"

Evening in Paris: Scent Has Faded, Memories Linger

A mystery woman has asked us to assist in turning up some Evening in Paris perfume.

Her identity will be a mystery because sales clerks all over Little Rock have left this shopper feeling like a retread.

"When I ask for Evening in Paris, they don't know what I'm talking about."

The mystery woman has made many telephone calls.

"Half the clerks go away and come back saying, 'We ain't got no Night on the Town perfume.'"

Where is the enchantment of yesteryear?

"My mother had an old-fashioned dresser. When she wasn't around, I used to climb up on the stool to look at her Evening in Paris. That blue bottle!"

Hearing no sounds nearby in the house, the young mystery child unscrewed the lid and got an actual whiff. *Evening in Paris.* My!

She got the lid back on in a hurry, jumped down, and replaced the stool.

Or did she imagine all that?

Further Search for a Very Special Evening Out of Past

Mrs. James T. Fargo of West Memphis accuses us of filling the air with Evening in Paris perfume, and then walking off and leaving it.

She declares, "You can't do that! Has anyone found a store that sells Evening in Paris? For old times' sake, this Christmas they would make a million dollars!"

A lot of folks are looking.

This is from Ed Lumsden of DeWitt:

"While a junior in LRHS in the winter of 1928–29, I had a home date with a lovely young lady who lived out West Markham past Stifft Station.

"On the divan in front of her fireplace a fragrance made me fall deeply in love. She told me it was Evening in Paris.

"I was so in love that it lasted until the next summer when the bathing suits came out, which showed even more interesting things than perfume.

"Now it is impossible to find Evening in Paris, for I have tried many times in the past twenty-five years and the clerks treat me like I am nuts."

It is possible that they are concealing this dangerous fragrance in new sheep's clothing.

Mercedes Jacobsen of Little Rock recalls that as a high school girl in Whittier, California, she thought of Evening in Paris as the ultimate in alluring fragrances.

"I got mine at the Rexall Drugstore."

Now something strange has happened.

"Just lately we received in the Sunday paper a sample of shampoo called Finesse. Never one to pass up a free sample, I used it. Maybe it was my imagination, but for three days, until the scent faded away, I was reminded of Evening in Paris."

Ann Ganschow of Hot Springs will not forget that powerful aroma, along with something equally deadly called Blue Waltz.

"More than half a century ago it was a staple item at the five-and-ten—beautifully wrapped at Christmas time. No self-respecting twelve-year-old young lady would be 'caught dead' wearing it."

But Ann Ganschow wore it.

"My heart sank the Christmas my nine-year-old brother gave me, with pride and anticipation of my joy, a large bottle. It came in such nice big bottles and cost so little!

"I pretended to be delighted. Used every drop. To this day my brother and I are still good friends."

From Nancy Trice of Little Rock:

"My mother, Kay Montgomery in Huntsville, has a bottle. Yes! It is in that special *blue* bottle, and when I see it the childhood memories flood back.

"I, too, would sneak a smell and put a small amount behind each ear. It was splash-on, not spray, heaven forbid!"

That perfume bottle sits now where it sat then—"on an old dresser that is covered with a handmade, crocheted cover, surrounded by knickknacks, old bottles of ointments, etc.—perfect!"

Nancy Trice told her mother she wanted that bottle someday.

Mrs. Montgomery said, "What about the jewelry? Or the money, and the furniture?"

The one who had sneaked the whiffs, and put the dabs behind her ears, the little girl grown up said, no, the blue bottle would be enough.

They grew up in Cleburne County, Flora Cauthron and her brother Walter.

Mrs. Cauthron writes from Hot Springs:

"The Christmas I was ten and Walter was twelve, I found a bottle of Evening in Paris in our barn, taped to the inside of a wheelbarrow, which I suppose was hung up for the winter."

Flora asked her brother about the perfume. His face turned red.

"He told me he was going to give it to somebody. But if he didn't, I could have it if I kept my mouth shut."

Christmas passed. The perfume stayed in the wheelbarrow.

"I've had it more than forty years. I knew the person it was intended for, and four or five years ago told her the story and showed her the bottle. We cried a long time together."

Walter died in a car wreck when he was eighteen.

This is from Flora Mabrey of El Dorado:

"We crawled up on Mom's dresser stool so many times, it's a wonder we didn't get calluses on our knees."

Flora's mother conducted Evening in Paris smelling sessions, with three young sisters gathered closely.

"Everybody got the same whiff, and then the cap went back on. We were forbidden to open the Evening in Paris because it would evaporate. Of course we all sneaked into her room anyway."

There was the Christmas season that Flora Mabrey was ten.

"On New Year's Day the Evening in Paris got broken. Do you think for one minute that the sister who did that deed, getting perfume all over her, could stand with the others and avoid detection?"

Mrs. Mabrey says, no, the mystery woman wasn't dreaming.

"I still remember how my backside felt, halfway through January."

Olive B. Farrell of North Litle Rock:

"My brother-in-law worked in the factory making the perfume, and gave us bottles and bottles of it. The factory was in London, England.

"I cannot find the perfume in this country or in England."

From Corinne Nelson of Horatio:

"Since I am an avid collector of all kinds of items, especially old and older things, I happen to have some old Christmas boxes that contain the perfume, cologne, etc., that have never been opened.

"If you can put the reader who wants the cologne in touch with me, I will be glad to let her have some for about the cost I paid."

This is signed "Lady from Paris (Arkansas)":

"Yes, Mystery Woman, there is an Evening in Paris perfume. Or there was. You didn't just dream of that blue bottle on the dresser. It was a popular scent for decades, advertised in women's magazines, and beloved of young ladies with not much to spend on fripperies.

"In the 1940s the company, Bourjois, also made bath powder, face powder, rouge, and lipstick, as well as cologne and perfume, and sponsored a regular weekly radio show, 'Here's to Romance,' with Jim Ameche and Ray Block's orchestra."

But the world stopped being elegant and turned high hat.

"By the 1960s it had become synonymous with 'cheap perfume' and had become something of a joke. Discriminating women wouldn't have been caught dead wearing Evening in Paris.

"The bottles have become 'collectibles,' and now and then at a flea market or junk store a lucky collector finds another little blue bottle to treasure. A few years ago I paid five dollars for a tiny (and empty) blue bottle—more than we ever paid for a full one. What price nostalgia!"

Mrs. J.B. Tucker of Salem:
"Tell the mystery lady I have a four-piece set—purse-size perfume, sachet perfume, cologne, eau de toilette. This was a Christmas gift in 1952. My bottles are gold."

Mrs. Dennis Beavert, who once lived in Arkansas, telephoned from Washington, D.C.:
"In 1957, when I was in the seventh grade, I gave my best friend a bottle of Evening in Paris, bought at Woolworth's. I wanted to keep the perfume so badly, but it was a present for my friend.

"Her mother made her stop seeing me. She said that was perfume for poor people. After that, her mother wouldn't talk to my mother."

It was never the same for the mothers.

In three weeks the young friends were together again.

Taking Scent-imental Journey Renews Old Memories

Thanks to Jean Williams of Fort Smith, we have here a bottle of Blue Waltz perfume, the genuine thing in its heart-shaped container, ⅝ fluid ounces, $1.49 plus tax at the Ben Franklin store.

We have passed the Blue Waltz beneath the noses of discerning associates, making them participants in a fragrance challenge.

Reactions have varied.

"That's elegant."

"Wow! That would gag a goat!"

It is obvious that Jean Williams herself never removed the perfume bottle cap.

She says, "Since it's all your fault for bringing up some of those long-buried mental scenes of one's childhood—here it is! *Do not return it under any circumstances.*"

This Valentine season we are proud of our bottle of Blue Waltz, and whatever that is floating around in there, if not ambergris, then surely some other whale part.

On three separate corners of her stationery, Audrey Stanley of North Little Rock has provided distinctive fragrances.

In the upper left-hand corner is Blue Waltz, labeled by smeary letters over a dab of the actual stuff.

In the upper right corner is Ben Hur. Put your nose up there.

Down in the lower left-hand corner is Evening in Paris.

Audrey Stanley's signature, having absorbed a large whiff of each, is at the lower right of the page.

"On this page I have put examples of the fragrances to 'stir yer memories.' Some of the bottles have sediment in them; however, I prefer to think of it as *sentiment.*"

From Thelma Johnson of Ashdown:

"Evening in Paris was so elegant that we kids couldn't afford it. Instead, we settled for Ben Hur, ten cents a bottle. Ben Hur was a shade below Evening in Paris but quite above

Blue Waltz, status-wise.

"Even during the Depression we could afford to be snobs, you know, if nothing else."

Years ago, on her twelfth Christmas, Ann Ganschow of Hot Springs got a bottle of Blue Waltz from her nine-year-old brother, Phil.

Phil's chest swelled, and Ann's heart sank. But she managed to use every drop of the perfume, and they remained good friends.

We reported this back before Christmas. Ann sent the clipping to Phil, who lives in Chicago.

Now she has a new, very old bottle of Evening in Paris, which probably belonged to Phil's wife, a native of Altus.

The perfume came with this note:

"Just a bit of nostalgia, and since you hillbillies down in Rebel country cannot find any of this fine stuff, I just thought I'd help out. Your brother and still friend (I hope), Phil."

James W. Hartford of Diamondhead writes a poem about how it was when, back in Kenosha, Wisconsin, his dad gave his mother a bottle of Evening in Paris for Christmas:

"Mom reached for the derby still on Dad's head,/ and with a great rip gave the brim a new bed;/ the dome of the hat stood proud in its place,/ but brim now rested round his neck like a lace."

In their Rexall store in a college town in Iowa, Lois B. Johnson and her husband had a large gift and cosmetics department.

Mrs. Johnson writes from Horseshoe Bend:

"By far the largest single selling line was Evening in Paris all year round but peaking at Christmas. On Christmas Eve the clerks left at 6:00 p.m. and the bosses would hang around, certain that all the young swains and dilatory businessmen would come hurrying in to make last-minute purchases.

"At that hour price was no object, and the big royal blue and silver boxes full of talc, perfume, cologne, soap, etc., sold like hotcakes."

Lois Johnson recalls those years for a special reason.

"I have a warm glow in my heart when I remember; for all those sales made it possible for me to move to Arkansas."

Spurned Gift Comes Back
Mysteriously at Christmas

In 1940, when he graduated from North Little Rock High School, John Harold Reeves went into the Economy Drugstore at Fourth and Main Streets and bought a present for his sweetheart, Virginia Walker.

John Harold Reeves was no piker. He plunked down a dollar bill—one big one—for a bottle of Evening in Paris perfume.

The woman in the drugstore wrapped the elegant gift, and John Harold went to Virginia Walker's house.

She might as well have unwrapped a tarantula.

"Not Evening in Paris!" she groaned.

John Harold Reeves couldn't believe it.

Virginia Walker said, "I can't stand the way that smells."

The big spender grabbed the gift and declared, all right, see if he ever gave her any more Evening in Paris perfume!

"I'll take the damn thing back."

Take that incident and throw in World War II.

Departing for flight school, John Harold was big about it. He told Virginia Walker, "If you'll wait around here till I get back, I'll marry you."

Whatever she replied didn't make any sense.

John Harold Reeves said, talking to himself, "All right, then, I don't care what you do!"

They were married near the end of the war, on May 24, 1945.

"Where is Mama's perfume?"

Nobody remembers just what year it started. It was twenty-five or thirty years ago.

Under the Reeveses' Christmas tree on Skyline Drive a mystery package appeared. Inside was the Evening in Paris perfume bought for one dollar at the Economy Drugstore.

It turned out that John Harold had not taken the damn thing back after all.

Again, the Christmas after that the unused perfume showed up under the tree. And the next Christmas, too—

every Christmas, year after year, in a large box, or a small box, always elegantly wrapped—"Which one of these is Mama's perfume?"

Across two generations, the Evening in Paris refused to evaporate.

He read in the newspaper that people were looking for Evening in Paris. Old-time affairs of the heart.

Last week John Harold Reeves got out his perfume, the bottle he always gets back on Christmas Day, the minute after his high school sweetheart unwraps it.

He took the Evening in Paris out into the Christmas marketplace.

At home that evening, Virginie Walker Reeves was told by her husband, "I sold the perfume today."

She said, "You didn't."

He said, "I got ten dollars for it from a woman at the drugstore."

The one who in forty-three years had not touched a drop of the perfume shook her head and said, "You didn't."

Which, of course, he didn't.

A mystery box, getting older, will be under the tree again.

Virginia Reeves says, "He wouldn't sell that perfume at any price."

And if he did?

"I'd kill him."

Powerful Essence Harder to Hide Than Orange Socks

Mary Kay Burnside of Fayetteville complains that our recurring discussion of perfumes ignores some power fragrances worn by young men during her teenaged years.

"My brother, for one, soaked himself with a concoction called 'Lilac' something, and went around smelling like the flowers of spring."

Naturally, Mary Burnside's brother denied it.

"Me?" he said, taking offense at the suggestion.

But it was harder to hide than orange socks, which he also wore on dress-up occasions.

Lilacs were everything.

"Our school bus barely touched the pavement. By the time everyone got on in the morning, especially the football boys, we were all riding along on a cloud. I don't know how Mr. Sims, our bus driver, stood it, except he had some pretty fancy stuff on his hair."

Mary Kay Burnside's point is that not everything you smelled was Blue Waltz or Ben Hur or Evening in Paris.

The inspiration came from the barbershop.

"You want this combed wet or dry?" the barber asked.

Only a fool, paying twenty cents for a haircut, would take less than was available. But with a certain detachment.

"Might as well make it wet."

Which brought out the Lucky Tiger.

Lucky Tiger was a blend of creosote and Dr. Pepper. In other words, it was elegant.

The barber shook this tonic onto a customer's head like he was shaking pepper sauce. It ran down around the ears. The barber put the tonic bottle down, made a vise of his hands, and pushed everything back toward the top of the head, cutting off the blood and leaving the customer in an exotic state of mind.

People have not looked or felt that good since then. If they did, you would see more orange socks.

A man asked us recently whether we knew somebody named Theo A. Koch.

The answer was, yes, we knew Koch. We went to school with him. Or if it wasn't school, then it was the Army. From somewhere we knew Koch, had known him for years.

Then it dawned on us that Theo A. Koch was the fellow who used to sit on the third-base line at old Travelers Field, hollering at opposing players who came in from Atlanta and Birmingham and New Orleans.

Yes, that was Theo A. Koch, a great baseball fan.

But this man said no.

"You don't know Koch," he said. "You just think you know him. Everybody thinks he knows Koch."

He explained.

"Theo A. Koch is the name you see when you're sitting in the barber chair, and the barber pushes your head forward to get at your neck, and you're looking down at your feet. That name down there on the footrest, between your shoes, it's Theo A. Koch."

She writes from Russellville, still hiding from her father.

"All these notes about the perfume made me recall my first lipstick. It was Tangee *natural*. They also had a red-red, but I didn't get to wear that. I barely got to wear the natural that was supposed to 'turn to your own true color.'"

On her it turned pale orange.

"I recall one day when a few of us girls walked to town. As soon as we got out of sight of our homes, one of the girls got out her red-red lipstick. We all put it on and thought we were about as grown as we'd ever be, and about as sultry.

"We had walked only a few blocks when we met my dad. It was too late to wipe it off. But off it came before he left us."

She keeps her name a secret.

"Daddy will see this and know, anyway!"

For Hair, More Than a Little Dab'll Do Ya

From Faye Daugherty of Heber Springs:

"Your essay on Lucky Tiger hair tonic reminded me of how well-groomed young men used to be recognized as they waited along Highway 65 for the bus to take them to school in Conway."

Faye Daugherty's older brother, Ralph, was one of these well-groomed young men.

"The last thing Ralph did before going out to the school bus was fix his hair, applying just the right mixture of hot water and Brilliantine."

On cold mornings it was a sight.

"When the temperature was near freezing, Ralph waited for the bus with steam coming off of his head. His hands were steaming, too, but they were in his pockets."

Half the boys who rode the school bus on winter mornings had rose-scented steam billowing from their heads.

"They made the insides of the windows fog over. We would have smelled like a rose garden, if it hadn't been for all that sausage in the lunches."

Proper grooming required leadership.

This is from Ken Parker, a Little Rock public relations man:

"My father used Stag hair oil. It was red, smelled like roses, and came in a squatty rectangular bottle. On Sundays and other special days, when my father would comb my hair, he would douse it with Stag hair oil."

Dousing was just the beginning.

"To make sure it had permeated the pores of my scalp, he would soak a towel in water as hot as his hands could stand, which was considerably warmer than my scalp could stand, and wrap the towel around my head. With the oil properly soaked into my head, he then would proceed to part and comb my hair."

An elegant head called for elegant clothes.

"When one's hair was properly oiled, steamed, and

combed, it was time to put on a rayon slack suit.

"Remember them? The 'suit' consisted of a pair of slacks and a matching short-sleeved shirt designed to be worn outside the slacks.

"These slack 'suits' were comfortable, but they did have one disadvantage. The rayon turned purple during the winter months, probably because of natural gas fumes in the house.

"When spring came around, everyone wore purple until he could afford to buy a new slack suit."

Journeys

A Scenic Run That Would Work Up an Appetite

ASHEVILLE, NORTH CAROLINA—It is just after sunup in the Great Smokies. Outside the Holiday Inn, Asheville East, the heads of early-appearing travelers are wrapped in low-hanging clouds.

It is these clouds that a young man is explaining to his young wife.

"That's how you know when you're right next to the ocean," the young man explains. "The moisture content of the clouds."

They drove in late yesterday, with their Oklahoma plates—from Stillwater—smudges of "Just Married" messages still evident on the new Toyota.

But morning has broken. Now on the parking lot they are warming up, running in place, dressed in matching new outfits, with matching blue and white running shoes.

Being from Oklahoma has uniquely qualified the bridegroom in coastal meteorology.

"You see how those clouds are shooting across there?"

She nods intently, jogging in place. Pad, pad, pad, pad.

"That dark part under the clouds," he notes. "It's practically solid water. Just off the Atlantic."

These clouds happen to be hurrying from west to east.

The bride nods intently. Pad, pad, pad, pad.

"How about it?" her husband says earnestly. "Are you about warmed up enough?"

She nods.

The bridegroom turns to an early-arriving motel employee. "How about it?" Pad, pad, pad, pad. "We have time, don't we, to run down to the ocean and back before breakfast?"

The motel employee says that depends on how late they like their eggs.

"To the ocean and back from here, that's right at eight hundred miles."

Personally, we are dashing on to Norfolk, Virginia, home

of the world's largest naval base. A personal matter must be discussed with the commanding officer of the destroyer *Caron.*

Inside the motel we have just finished our free breakfast, courtesy of Holiday Inn.

Breakfast came free with the sixty-one-dollar room.

It was informative, listening to two local men, stopping off for coffee on their way to work.

"What I don't understand is this," said the first man, "if they're going to have a huge marijuana bust, a nationwide crackdown, why would you spread it all over the front page ahead of time? And all over the TV? 'Here I come, ready or not.'"

The second man drank coffee. He said, "Yeah, I seen that."

The first man went on, "On the other hand, you have to assume the officials know exactly what they were doing. Tipping their hand for the maximum advantage."

The second man agreed, yes, you would have to assume that.

The first man said, "On the other hand, if the officials knew so much about what they were doing, why did they get so confused when it rained?"

The second man drank coffee. He said, "Yeah, I seen that part, too."

Travelers on Interstate 40 in North Carolina are urged by billboards to "Buy Towels by the Pound."

It is difficult to assimilate.

"I'll take three pounds of towels, please. The ones that don't say Holiday Inn on them."

Joggers from Oklahoma would go by too fast to see the billboards.

So we are pressing on to Norfolk.

Aboard the destroyer *Caron* is a young radioman from Little Rock, Paul Allbright.

It is one thing to go to San Diego for boot camp.

It is another to run down the Eastern Seaboard, with America in sight.

Or even drop through the Canal Zone, for a look at the

coast of Nicaragua.

But now they are talking something else. They are talking relieving another destroyer in the Mediterranean.

That is across a lot of water.

To places with foreigners on every street corner.

For one place, Lebanon.

We will talk with the commanding officer of the *Caron*. At the last minute he will put this child off his boat.

Price Estimates Sought to Dry-dock Radioman

NORFOLK, VIRGINIA—We have here a foldup map of Norfolk, Virginia, home of the largest naval base in the civilized world.

The map arrived in a manila envelope, mailed by a young radioman, Paul Allbright.

Although only twenty-one, Allbright apparently is in charge of the destroyer *Caron,* and virtually everything else in the Atlantic.

His letter instructs, "Dad, be sure to bring this map when you come. You'll need it to get around."

There is an apology.

"Sorry I had to cut the map up. That's the only way I could get it back into the envelope."

Sleep well, America.

In its front window at the huge shopping center called Military Circle, a legal firm lists its prices for various services offered to Norfolk residents and visitors. These services and prices are as follows:

"Divorce Uncontested—$175

"Simple Will—$35

"Bankruptcy—$200

"Advice—$15"

There is something undemocratic about the high cost of going broke.

But this list of services is significant for what it leaves out.

For example, how much does it cost to buy a young radioman from Little Rock off a warship preparing to sail for the Mediterranean?

Right now the destroyer *Caron* sits high in dry dock.

There is no secret about this. With a pass and an escort, you can walk right up to the *Caron.* Touch it.

"They're doing some work on the screws," says our escort. He is the young radioman, Paul Allbright, who should be at home eating pancakes with a spoon and talking to his skateboard.

139

Screws? How could screws matter to this hulking thing, longer than a football field?

"Dad, the screws are the propellers."

He walks over. Shows us the screws.

They are taller than the radioman.

It is time to call this whole thing off.

For the record, speaking of pancakes, at a pancake emporium back in Winston–Salem, North Carolina, nobody was smoking a Winston.

Also, nobody was smoking a Salem.

During a period covering forty-five minutes, no customer of the pancake emporium in Winston–Salem lighted up.

It could be that blueberry pancakes go better with just a peench of wintergreen.

We asked the cashier whether more people in Winston–Salem probably smoked Winstons or Salems.

She said, "Are you crazy? I don't know *anybody* who smokes *anything*."

The traffic artery called Military Highway changes its name somewhere along the way to Admiral Taussig Boulevard, which in turn turns into the world's largest naval base.

Our motel is alongside this artery.

Tossing and turning, we have awakened in the dead of night, around 11:15, rehearsing our speech to the commanding officer of the destroyer *Caron.*

What is on television?

Imagine our surprise, and delight, on turning on the set and being greeted by none other than Paul Eels.

A friendly face from home! The Channel 7 sports man, himself, right here in Norfolk! We might even have passed on the highway.

But no. Apparently Paul Eels is here on videotape only. He is offering us, the viewer, a telephone, handing it practically right out of the TV screen, inviting us to call up and order some Craftmagic or Craftmatic bedding. Whichever, it makes for an outstanding night's sleep.

The idea itself helps do the trick.

But a person does not drive 1,060 miles to get a night's sleep.

We will point out to the commanding officer—what about Radioman Allbright's birthday? September 21. He usually has a few little friends over.

Then there will be Thanksgiving. Your radioman frequently dresses up like a turkey.

Where do you hang a Christmas stocking on the destroyer *Caron?*

Sir, you are talking about putting this warship to sea for a serious period of time, seven months, and sailing it far from the customary skies.

The radioman does not have our permission to go.

Navy Radioman's Reports Lack "The Right Stuff"

Numerous people have inquired into the whereabouts of a young Navy radioman, Paul Allbright, who late in August set sail from Norfolk, Virginia, for the Mediterranean Sea.

We attended that departure personally, to advise authorities that young Allbright was not the "right stuff" for their project—that, in fact, he could not take a shower without sinking the bathroom.

The destroyer *Caron* sailed anyway, with Radioman Allbright aboard.

News has come back across the Atlantic in a steady flow.

Unfortunately, only a cryptographer can understand it.

For example, after the *Caron* left port at Nice, France, Radioman Allbright confided in a letter, "You would not believe what some of the guys did in Monaco."

Apparently naval security is at stake.

How else would you interpret "Va Va Va Voom!"?

And Italy, no less than France, was shrouded in mystery.

"Those [scratch-overs] in Naples—they were out of sight!"

In a subsequent letter, the radioman explained to his grandmother that what got scratched over was "pasta dishes."

Only from the Strait of Gibraltar was the reporting vividly detailed.

The destroyer *Caron* passed The Rock at midnight, visibility dead solid zero, everything dark as three feet down a bear's throat.

Radioman Allbright exposed an entire role of color film, shooting off both sides of the fantail—he thinks—to make certain nothing went unrecorded.

It is only just now, within recent hours, that the most gratifying report of all has arrived from the Mediterranean.

The letter was mailed from Haifa, Israel.

"Dad,

"I went on a tour, to Jerusalem and Bethlehem.

"I saw where Jesus was born, and where they kept Him before the resurrection.

"I was trying not to do anything wrong while we were there."

"Easy Day's Drive" Translates as Eleven Hours, Forty Minutes

GULF SHORES, ALABAMA—The skilled traveler arrives at this place called Gulf Shores through a series of fortuitous mistakes.

"You must go to Dauphin Island, Alabama," friends insisted, planning this vacation for us.

Dauphin Island?

"It's an easy day's drive. An absolute must."

So the thing was resolved.

The travel plan was drawn scientifically, using a wax pencil on the map of Southern states.

In Louisiana, turn left. At Mississippi, turn right. Where the road runs into the Gulf of Mexico, turn left.

In no time we would be on Dauphin Island, off the coast of Alabama.

"That's on the western tip of Mobile Bay," friends said. "Right across the bay is Fort Morgan and Gulf Shores. It's only about three miles."

The sign outside the post office in Transylvania, Louisiana, flashed "See Our Bat and Dracula T-Shirts."

They must sell a lot of postmarks in Transylvania.

The sign in front of somebody's house in Prentiss, Mississippi, said, "Garden Fresh Eggs."

It was approximately here that the disorientation set in.

Never mind the garden fresh eggs. What were we doing in Prentiss, Mississippi?

The wax marks on the map of Southern states showed that in the process of turning right at Mississippi we had kept on turning right, doing such a good job of it, so that up there ahead lay Monroe, Louisiana.

This was hardly the plan.

The man at the Chevron station explained, "I could tell you how to get back to where you thought you were, but you'd probably get lost."

Determined to avoid that, we set off from Prentiss in several directions and in no time pulled across the causeway to Dauphin Island, Alabama.

In darkness the message pinned to the screen door of the motel office was not immediately readable. Then the words murked out beneath the light of a forty-watt bulb, pallid survivor of the tourist season: "BE BACK SOON."

What was soon? Ten minutes? Next week? The first of the year?

Morning has burst on the sugar-white sand of Gulf Shores.

The sand sparkles out to meet the surf, which comes to make the union gently.

Beyond is the blue-green water, nothing more, filling the eye entirely beneath a high and cloudless sky.

Cloudless?

Out there at a distance of about four hundred miles, upwardly, is what might be a sugar-white cloud, the size of a dime. It is quickly gone, so who can say?

The average temperature here is 68.8 degrees. This Indian Summer morning we are ten degrees above that. It would not seem gentlemanly to complain.

Dauphin Island, which friends say we must see, is back there across Mobile Bay, a distance of only three miles from point to point, if you drive your car on water.

We crept off Dauphin Island under cover of darkness, as we had crept on, and driving on various roads looped around the bay, arriving here at Gulf Shores in no time.

For the record, "no time" from Little Rock was eleven hours and forty minutes behind the wheel, which fixes the alert traveler more or less permanently in the stage-exiting posture of Groucho Marx.

It will be the perfect posture for sitting down in an inner tube and joining our friend, Julia Cordelia, who is out there in the water now, inner-tubing, a painted scow upon a painted ocean.

The beach is ours, except for a family of three.

The man, nearing sixty, is surf casting.

The woman sits on the sand with their son, he being full-grown but not in every way. The man–son wears a baseball cap, a T-shirt, and blue jeans rolled above the ankles.

He walks about the sand barefooted, pulling a large beach ball with a cord tied to one of his wrists.

Photographs Preserve Historic Moment Near Mobile

FORT MORGAN, ALABAMA—Here in the museum on the point below Mobile a woman is explaining how it was that day in August 1864 when Admiral David Farragut jumped up and, using sailor language, shouted his undying words—"Damn the torpedoes! Full speed ahead!"

This woman is a visitor, like the rest of us, but it is apparent that she knows her naval history.

"Admiral Farragut was docked right out here," she explains, indicating a spot on a large glass-encased map of Mobile Bay.

Listeners move in a half-step closer to get a better view of her finger.

A small voice in the group observes, "He wasn't docked."

The explainer looks down at the voice, a boy of about nine. She begs his pardon.

"Admiral Farragut wasn't docked," the boy says. "When you're ten miles out in the ocean you can't be docked. There isn't any dock out there."

We all take a half-step back.

The woman says, "It is just an expression."

She turns again to the map to explain the celebrated event.

"We are at this location, Mobile Point. Across the bay there, a distance of three miles, is Dauphin Island. The two points guarded Mobile Bay against Union forces, and before that against enemies from other nations."

The group moves in a half-step closer. We take a picture of the woman's finger, pointing at the map.

"Admiral Farragut lay offshore in his flagship *Hartford*. *Hartford* was not ten miles out in the ocean, as some suggest. Farragut held approximately this position, commanding a view of the bay."

His mission?

"He was to capture the defenses of Mobile."

Outside the museum at Fort Morgan there is shouting of some sort.

It sounds as though somebody is hollering, "Here comes the *Lexington!* Here comes the *Lexington!*"

In historic settings such as this the quickened imagination plays strange tricks.

Inside we resume the Battle of Mobile Bay.

"Of course, Admiral Farragut's forces already had the bay blockaded," the woman explains. "But right along here"—she takes her finger again to the map, and we photograph the finger from a different angle—"right along here near the coastline was a line of piles, leaving a narrow channel for blockade runners."

The small boy, directly in front of the narrator, folds his arms.

"As the affair began, Admiral Farragut's officers advised him that they were under dire threat of Confederate torpedoes. That the deadly weapons were, in fact, bearing down on them with great speed at that instant."

She pauses, withdraws her finger, and holds it motionless in the air. "We all know what Admiral Farragut's reply was."

Our group says in union—"Damn the torpedoes"—a historic moment which we were able to photograph right there at the map.

"It wasn't that way," the small boy says, his arms still folded.

Our narrator begs his pardon.

"Self-propelled torpedoes hadn't been invented. What they had was big old cans of gunpowder. Like mines. They floated them toward the targets, or pulled them around behind boats."

Our narrator, tight-lipped, declares, "It is only an expression. Young man, are you saying Admiral Farragut didn't shout, 'Damn the torpedoes'?"

The young man says, "He probably didn't."

The door of the museum flies open and somebody shouts, "You're missing it! You're missing it! There goes the *Lexington!*"

We all dash out, crossing in front of the old fort, making camera adjustments on the run, arriving near the water's edge through a field of stickly burrs, collecting a harvest of those around the ankles.

Now she is steaming away in the distance. But right out

147

there is the exact spot where three minutes ago the carrier *Lexington* sped by, not four hundred yards offshore, passing over the exact spot, or thereabouts, where Admiral Farragut shouted whatever he did, if he shouted anything.

Fortunately, we have pictures of a woman's finger to prove it.

Somewhere Beyond All the Rain Must Be the Ocean

SANTA ROSA ISLAND, FLORIDA—The woman in the motel office said that right here outside our back door, not fifty paces across the white sand, or sixty paces at the most—right out there is the Gulf of Mexico.

She might be right.

We were checked in, after all, at a place called El Mar, "the sea."

And something is roaring out there, roaring and booming, in a manner that we have heard ocean water behave as it comes ashore.

But being checked in at nightfall, in a pouring rain, it is impossible to see ten paces out there, much less fifty or sixty, press as one might his nose against the sliding glass door. We cannot even see the sand.

So at the moment we are relying on the motel woman's integrity and good judgment. The big water must be out there.

This pouring rain is a blessing. It keeps a person from concentrating on the cold.

Somebody inquired in the motel office, "What is the temperature out there?"

The man behind the counter had not noticed any temperature.

"We don't sell weather," he explained.

It will take us awhile to figure out what he meant, if we ever do.

His wife said, "It must be in the fifties."

Back home in Arkansas when it gets down to these Florida "fifties" we go out and wrap the hydrant.

"You should have been here at Christmas," the woman in the office said. "The weather was terrible."

This whole thing is disorienting. Credit two days of driving, skirting flood waters in Louisiana and Mississippi.

To get to El Mar we have driven out two barrier reefs from Pensacola. The town is back there somewhere, in some direction, but its name keeps coming and going in odd ways, first as Pensacola, then as Pepsi Cola, once as Pocatello, and most recently as Pocahontas.

We do not stand up to long drives the way we used to.

To confuse matters further, we have made no sense out of the last roadway sign visible before darkness and the rain closed in.

The sign said: "UNLAWFUL TO PICK SEA OATS."

It is beyond us who would want to pick sea oats.

The person who travels with us says, "Somebody with a seahorse."

But then here it is, in the National Park Service literature:

"Barrier islands are special places. They appear permanent and static but in fact are continually changing, moving parallel to the mainland and toward or away from it. They buffer the mainland from storms, but storms may cause a particular island to disappear or split in two. Or storms may push a dune line clear across an island as Hurricane Frederic did in 1979 on parts of Santa Rosa Island."

Sea oats, their root systems, hold barrier islands together.

In all likelihood, out there in the darkness somebody is harvesting sea oats right now.

So an early turn-in, to be fresh for tomorrow.

The man on television reports that the temperature at Pensacola is forty-one degrees, and that rain is expected for the next five days.

The Gulf of Mexico should be out of its banks by morning.

The man on television reports something else interesting.

It seems that a man being detained in a Pensacola jail has received a ten-year sentence for tampering with police evidence.

How the detainee tampered was, he sat there in jail and cut a bullet out of his leg and disposed of it, thereby frustrating further investigation of something.

Welcome to the Sunshine State.

These early notes in no way reflect a sagging spirit on the part of the traveler.

After all, we have just got here, if we are here.

And there is concrete evidence that when we wake up in the morning the big water will, in fact, be out there.

The evidence is not literally concrete. For now it is only sand. Somehow we have managed to track a large dune of it into the bed.

St. Augustine Must Feel Young After This Explosion

SANTA ROSA ISLAND, FLORIDA—Morning has broken, and the beach is littered with blue things.

"What are those blue things?"

The question comes with a shout, over the booming of surf, and the pounding of rain on umbrellas.

Strewn here and there on the sand, the blue things could be large, empty sandwich bags, crescent-shaped, inflated almost to popping.

"Stay away from that!" somebody shouts. "That's a Portuguese man-of-war. Especially if it has those things hanging down."

The Portuguese man-of-war is any of several oceanic hydrozoans of the genus *Physalia*, having a large bladderlike structure by which it is buoyed up and from which are suspended numerous processes.

The float length of the man-of-war (the sandwich baggie) might be eight inches, and the processes (those things hanging down) can go forty to sixty feet.

These are not creatures in which God concentrated great beauty.

And now, washed up on the beach, their work is done, whatever the work was.

From out of nowhere, from behind a dune, a youth dashes across the sand, leaps high into the air, and comes down with both feet on a Portuguese man-of-war. In a posthumous salute, the former creature explodes like a pistol shot.

The youth walks away, hands jammed into his pockets, going in no particular direction.

Yesterday's rain is gone. Today's rain has arrived with a vengeance.

A man in the motel office explains, "Weather is really nothing more than a state of mind."

He sees virtues in weather. Especially a cold Florida rain.

"It gives you an opportunity to do things you hadn't planned."

Somebody asks, "Like what?"

The motel man does not know like what. It takes a little time to plan unplanned activities.

"That's the beauty of it," he says. "It's up to the individual."

Parts of a boat have washed ashore on Santa Rosa Island. Boat parts and boat supplies—a milk carton, the lid from a Styrofoam cooler, what appears to have been a jug of vinegar.

On television they are talking about what might have happened.

A reporter at the scene says intently, "It is not yet known whether a mishap was involved here, or whether someone went out and tried to sink the craft on purpose."

From the studio, the anchorperson asks, "Tell us, Mike, does it appear to have been a mishap, or did someone try to sink the craft on purpose?"

Mike thinks it over and fires back, his voice rising to compete with a helicopter, "That is not yet known."

Somebody wonders why the beach at Santa Rosa is so white, when other beaches along the Gulf Coast are not so white.

It is scientifically obvious to us, as a one-time geology student, that any sand that gets rained on this much is going to stay as clean as a hound's tooth. Especially when you throw in a jug of vinegar.

But they say, no, that is not the explanation.

This is quartz sand, washed down over the centuries as weathered rock from northern uplands. That made the sand white to begin with.

What keeps it white is the abrupt fall of the ocean floor just a few feet from the shore. It is virtually impossible for shells to wash up in large numbers and discolor the beach.

So if somebody had in mind looking for shells, he needn't go through with it, if it ever stops raining.

That's the beauty of planned and unplanned activities. It's up to the individual.

Now get this brochure history:

"Pensacola, the first settlement in the United States, 'the place where it all began,' was first settled on August 14, 1559.

The settlement predates St. Augustine, Florida, the oldest permanent U.S. settlement, by six years."

First a Portuguese man-of-war explodes. And now there goes St. Augustine.

"Sundown Ferry" an Ideal Spot to Wait for Last Boat

He calls himself simply "Josh," and he writes from the lake country of Baxter County, in far north Arkansas.

"Pardon me while I have an old man's thought or two about the passing of the ferry from Lake Norfork. Understand, I would not get in the way of progress."

Those shores have been joined by a bridge.

What is passing?

"They have called it the *free* ferry and *Henderson* ferry and *that damn* ferry, me included as a younger man, being eager to be about my business, whatever a young man's business was."

Whatever it was, that business changed.

"I was waiting for that damn ferry, near sundown on an early spring day, when I met the girl I married. We skipped rocks, and laughed, and that was it."

The ferry got a forever-new name. Sundown Ferry.

"For as long as she lived, the question as we drove there was not whether we'd have to wait for the ferry, but whether we'd get to."

On the crossing they never talked, but stood at opposite rails, alone together.

Then drawing to shore, returning to the car:

"I love you."

"I love you, too."

Not every time. It is a long voyage, thirty-one years.

"But even when the words weren't there, by the time we got across they were almost there again."

Josh would not stand in the way of progress. Maybe somebody will meet at the foot of the new bridge.

"In November she took another boat and went on without me. I don't know when that boat will be back for me, but I'm waiting. And I will run to meet it."

As a youngster we once fished from the ferry at Henderson, waiting for the boat to leave for crossing.

This was our first real casting "outfit," a short, stiff metal rod with reel attached, bought new for maybe fifty cents at The Ramey Company on the square in Mountain Home (although probably not bought at all, because didn't our people own the store?).

There was no monofilament. With fishing line not much smaller than a finger, we attached a genuine artificial lure, a River Runt made of wood, tying it on with a bow knot.

That first cast produced a monumental backlash—a "bird's nest," as we would learn to call it. Somehow the mess came untangled.

The second cast shot out from the ferry, plopping the wooden River Runt fifteen feet away, in ten inches of clear shore water.

A sunfish attacked the lure, and somebody started yelling. We learned later that it was us.

"You can't fish from the ferry"—the man in overalls came toward us, walking in heavy shoes, pointing his finger. He was the man in charge.

High excitement, infused with shame, turns your face red.

"That's all right, son"—his voice was softer as he got there, and the man in charge took his finger down. "It's just the rule. We can't fish from the ferry."

In the clear water, the sunfish yanked with annoyance at the River Runt, more than half his size.

"Don't allow him any slack, son."

We didn't. Given that approval, we cranked on the reel with such velocity that the fish planed across the water, bouncing and skipping like a riderless ski rope trailing a tow boat. If he has lived this long, that sunfish is still dizzy.

"He's a nice one," the ferryman said, engulfing the great fish in one hand, taking him gently from the hook with the other.

For a long moment he held the fish, letting us look. Then he dropped him back into Lake Norfork.

We watched the spot where the fish went in until the ferryboat pulled away.

That was a long time ago, before anybody in his right mind visualized shooting an actual bridge across so enormous a body of water.

You might as well have talked about shooting a man to the moon.

But the memory of it is fixed.

It would be a good spot to wait for the last boat.

The Last One Called

HOT SPRINGS, ARKANSAS—The benches were damp along the promenade above Central Avenue Wednesday. At mid-morning, when their regular occupants had not appeared, the squirrels came in a hop along the brick walk, quizzically, to take their morning peanuts from a stranger.

For the second day, the weather was not just right; nothing severe, but the dampness lay against the benches and the walks, causing the new leaf-fall to cling.

A splendid Indian summer might have slipped away almost overnight.

"Have you seen Fred?"

He must have been eighty, the questioner. At a fast shuffle he had come along the walk, sweatered, capped, and wearing black rubber overshoes. Under one arm he had a checkerboard, wrapped in laundry bag plastic.

We guessed we had not seen Fred.

"He's the big, tall fellow, stooped over, and wears a cap like mine. It's sort of our trademark."

No, we had not seen him.

The checkers player started to sit down on the bench but changed his mind, looking up and down the walk.

"He hasn't been feeling good—said he might make a trip back to Minnesota. Wouldn't you know it's a damn poor time for that?"

Down on Central the horns were honking, but all that was invisible beneath the trees.

"If you see Fred, tell him his partner is looking for him."

He chose the direction of Reserve Street and headed up the long gentle incline, straying from center but at a pace strong enough to send fat pigeons dodging off to both sides.

Thirty yards away he sat down on a bench in thin sunlight, resting the checkerboard on one knee.

A young couple came by, strolling and feeding the squirrels and pigeons. Then an old man, walking slowly with an umbrella cane.

The checkers player stood and watched the old man approach and when he drew even, stopped him. There was a conversation in the middle of the walk, the checkers player raising one hand above his head, no doubt to show Fred's height.

When the man with the cane started on up the slope, Fred's partner headed back down.

"You see, I don't know his whole name. Old Strayhorn knew him, but he's gone. Old Rosso knew him, but he's gone. They would have known how to get in touch with him."

The horns were honking and the puny sunlight was coming and going.

"You see, he didn't show up Monday and he didn't show up yesterday. Now he's not showing up again today."

We thought Fred might show up soon.

"No," he said, shaking his head. "I don't think so." He headed down the hill with his checkerboard.

We remember from ancient times standing under a streetlight, one-handing a baseball into the air and trying to decide—was it really best, being the last kid called home before dark?

CHARLES ALLBRIGHT has been a reporter, editorial writer and columnist for the *Arkansas Gazette* since 1955, except for seven years spent as a speechwriter for Governor Winthrop Rockefeller. He has written the *Gazette's* "Arkansas Traveler" column continuously since 1974.